OPPORTUNITIES IN
TRANSPORTATION
CAREERS

Adrian A. Paradis

Foreword by
Robert S. McIlwain
Group Publisher
Mass Transit

VGM Career Horizons
NTC/Contemporary Publishing Group

Library of Congress Cataloging-in-Publication Data

Paradis, Adrian A.
    Opportunities in transportation careers / Adrian A. Paradis ; foreword
by Robert S. McIlwain.
        p.   cm.
    Includes bibliographical references (p.).
    ISBN 0-8442-4682-4 (cloth)
    ISBN 0-8442-4683-2 (paper)
        1. Transportation—Vocational guidance—United States.   I. Title.
HE203.P28   1997
388'.023'73—dc21   96-47280
                                                                              CIP

Cover photographs: Upper left courtesy of Consolidated Freightways Corporation,
Menlo Park, California.
Upper right courtesy of United Airlines.
Lower left courtesy of Chicago Transportation Authority.
Lower right courtesy of New York Convention & Visitors Bureau.

Published by VGM Career Horizons
A division of NTC/Contemporary Publishing Group, Inc.
4255 West Touhy Avenue, Lincolnwood (Chicago), Illinois 60646-1975 U.S.A.
Printed in the United States of America
International Standard Book Number: 0-8442-4682-4 (cloth)
                                                          0-8442-4683-2 (paper)
99 00 01 02 03 04 VP 20 19 18 17 16 15 14 13 12 11 10 9 8 7 6 5 4 3 2

CONTENTS

ABOUT THE AUTHOR

Adrian A. Paradis was born in Brooklyn, New York, and graduated from Dartmouth College and Columbia University's School of Library Service. As a writer, businessman, vocational specialist, and researcher, he has published widely, with more than forty titles to his credit. He has covered subjects that range from banking to biographies, from public relations to religion, from vocational guidance to reference works, and from law to economics.

Mr. Paradis spent over twenty years as an officer of a major national corporation handling corporate matters, economic analysis, stockholder relations, corporate philanthropic contributions, security, and general administrative responsibilities. He lives in Sugar Hill, New Hampshire, where he serves as editor of Phoenix Publishing, a small firm that specializes in regional trade books and New England town histories.

FOREWORD

There is an axiom about planning a business: "The three most important things to consider are location, location, and location." Like so many of our clichés, this one has a strong foundation in truth. It might be rephrased to say: "Access to people, products, and services is essential to the success of any endeavor." Transportation provides that access.

It is impossible to consider the field of transportation without reflecting on its history. All over the world social and economic development has been profoundly affected, and often defined, by the easy flow of the people and products that fuel our engines of growth. Cities have developed next to ports or along land trading routes. Suburban residential areas grow where there is access to jobs and services. Manufacturing facilities are located where raw materials can be delivered and products shipped. Retail outlets succeed where they can be easily reached by customers. This pattern began with the invention of the wheel and continues to this day.

The long and rich history of the transportation industry can lend an unfortunate anachronistic quality to a career in the field. The notion of a career in transportation somehow conjures up visions of coverall-clad locomotive engineers, sweating mule skinners, or daring young men in their flying machines. As the Appian Way has evolved into today's superhighway, a career in transportation now demands technical and professional skills of the highest magnitude.

The transportation industry is unique among careers in that it holds opportunities for everyone. The complex and diverse nature of the business creates a demand for nearly every specialty. Salespeople and marketers; civil, electrical, and mechanical engineers; communications experts; lawyers; and environmentalists all have their roles to play.

The future of the industry is bright. While downsizing brought about by greater operating efficiencies has reduced the need for some specialties, others have developed to take their place. As the world economy grows, and as population centers become increasingly congested, the demand for efficient freight and passenger transportation services will grow proportionally. As a transportation professional, you can expect financial rewards ranging from adequate to exceptional, but perhaps the greatest reward will be the knowledge that you are a part of an industry that quite literally keeps the wheels of our economy turning and helps raise the overall quality of life.

Robert S. McIlwain
Group Publisher
Mass Transit

PREFACE

Transportation is not a series of unrelated activities but a truly remarkable and ever-developing industry that has always played an essential role in our nation's history and growth. The chapter arrangement in this third revision of *Opportunities in Transportation Careers* recognizes a logical progression in the development of transportation from the morning those first settlers landed on America's shore until today. Thus each type of transportation is introduced in order of its appearance on the North American continent, together with a brief sketch of its history in order to place it properly in the overall history of our nation.

Transportation brought the Pilgrims and other early immigrants to our shores, made subsequent settlement in New England possible, opened up the West, helped large cities expand, put an American on the moon, and today offers stable employment to more than 3,700,000 men and women in every part of the United States. This book covers the historical and contemporary story of transportation and the wide range of careers it now offers you.

CHAPTER 1

THE LURE OF THE WATER

OUR OCEANGOING HERITAGE

From man's earliest days, shipping has been important to his economic and social growth. Small boats could easily carry passengers and freight along the coastlines of oceans, seas, lakes, and rivers in preference to travel over land. The latter required cutting roads through forests and across deserts, often a difficult and dangerous undertaking, especially if hostile inhabitants were encountered. Little wonder, then, that civilization developed mostly along seacoasts and inland rivers.

At first this was true on the North American continent, too. Early explorers sailed along the New England coastline and farther south, some of them establishing tentative colonies on the edge of the forbidding forests. Were it not for those tiny ships manned by curious and courageous mariners who reached these shores, this vast continent might never have been discovered and settled.

Thus our oceangoing heritage traces back to those voyagers who reached these shores, who sailed here from Europe and subsequently traded along the Atlantic seaboard and down to the West Indies. Soon many early settlers became shipbuilders thanks to the unlimited source of lumber and good prospects of transatlantic trade with mother countries where markets for New World products were growing.

Although American privateers were active during the Revolutionary War, it was the French Fleet that contributed to the final British surrender at Yorktown. Realizing the need to build a strong navy, the new American Congress authorized construction of the U.S. *Constitution* (old "Ironsides"), a forty-four-gun frigate that took part in the Tripolitan War and the War of 1812 and today is enshrined in Boston harbor.

America has a proud heritage of ocean transportation. Following the War of 1812, the swift packet boats and merchant ships carried most of the coastal and transatlantic passenger and freight traffic. Gradually steamships were introduced, and an outstanding marine development was that of the famous Clipper ships, designed for speedy travel between the United States and China for the tea and opium trades.

With discovery of gold in California, gold seekers who wanted to avoid the dangerous overland trip from the east elected the ocean voyage, either around Cape Horn or shortening it by leaving the ships at the Isthmus of Panama, making their way across to the Pacific, and completing their journey by ship. California's growing population soon swelled the traffic and included all the rolling stock, rails, and equipment used to construct the western part of the transcontinental railroad. However, once the rails had met at Promontory Point, Utah, and trains started running from east to west, much of the former ocean freight and passenger business shifted to the rails. Following the Civil War, England's new steel ships gave her a wide advantage over other nations including the United States, which were slower to build similar merchant marine fleets (a nation's fleet of commercial ships). By the mid-1930s America's merchant marine had declined so far that Congress passed the Merchant Marine Act of 1936 to subsidize construction of a merchant marine and provide for appointment of a Maritime Commission to stimulate shipbuilding.

Soon the country greatly expanded its merchant marine to meet the needs of World War II, but that vast fleet proved unnecessary once peace returned. Transatlantic passenger traffic picked up again with the reappearance of luxurious liners, the best-known of which flew the colors of England, France, Holland, Italy, and the United States. After the late 1950s, however, jet airlines cut transatlantic travel times from four or five days to just hours, and by 1996 the only prestige ship still sailing from the United States was the *QE II,* which offered special inducement fares for travelers who wanted to sail one way and jet back. For those who craved an ocean voyage, numerous cruise ships offered luxurious accommodations on various itineraries. Meanwhile owners of many cargo ships had transferred their registries to countries such as Panama or Liberia, which assessed much lower taxes and had less stringent safety requirements.

NATIONAL MARITIME UNION

Now let's step back to 1936, specifically to Sunday, March 1, when the SS *California* put into San Pedro, California, her departure set for 6:00 the next morning. That afternoon the crew, which was from New York, held a meeting and agreed to demand equal pay with that being given the seamen who were working on the West Coast. It would mean $5 more a month for the deck and engine department crew, or $62.50 a month, and a monthly increase of $10 for stewards, giving them a monthly salary of $50. Early Monday morning Joe Curran, the crew's spokesman, delivered the ultimatum to the captain. Company response was immediate. A replacement crew was quickly recruited to take the place of the seamen who would certainly walk off the ship when their demands were refused.

This time was different, though. The crew refused to leave the ship or cast anchor. For three days the vessel remained tied up, the crew performing all its usual duties except to uncoil the heavy ropes restraining the ship.

"Mutiny!" and "Striking Seamen Face Charges of Mutiny" read the headlines. Editors and readers fumed at the strikers and especially at "mutineer" Curran. The strike became such a serious issue nationally, that on the third day Frances Perkins, secretary of labor, called from Washington to speak with Curran personally.

"You'll have to sail that ship out of there," she told the tough leader.

"Not until the crew gets some recognition as human beings," was Curran's answer.

After more conversation Mrs. Perkins finally asked: "Well, Joe, what is it that you want?"

By the time the conversation ended, Curran had promised to do his best to get the crew to sail the ship back to New York. For her part, the labor secretary promised to use her influence to make certain that none of the crew were "intimidated, coerced or persecuted" when they reached home port. As the ship made its way down the coast, the International Seamen's Union (ISU) and the shipowners negotiated a $5 monthly increase for sailors on the Atlantic and Gulf coasts. But the moment the *California* docked, her next sailing was canceled and the seamen were fired. In Washington the secretary of commerce wanted to bring mutiny charges against the crew, but President Roosevelt backed Mrs. Perkins's promise and they were not molested.

Now the smoldering fires of revolt burst into flame. When the $5 increase was approved, the ISU officials failed to press for an even more important demand: that all hiring be done through the union hall and that the agreement provide overtime pay. Heading the revolt against "indignity and exploitation" was able-bodied seaman, Joe Curran.

Joe was born in New York City in 1906. His father died when he was a small boy and he was boarded with a family in New Jersey. After finishing sixth grade he took a series of jobs and in 1922, at the age of sixteen, decided that he wanted to go to sea in a big ship. What he found below deck astonished him. In many ships the crews' quarters were filthy, rat-infested holes; food was often putrid; hours were excessively long; and the pay was minimal. Worse yet, for the privilege of working under these conditions, a person had to bribe those in charge of hiring seamen. Little wonder that sailors on all coasts were rebelling. Their union, the ISU, was doing little to help them, and many members even accused their union officials of participating in some of the unethical and illegal hiring practices.

The rest of the story can be found in the history books and the National Maritime Union's publication, *On a True Course, The Story of the National Maritime Union, AFL-CIO.* On May 3, 1937, the rank-and-file seamen held a mass rally in New York and founded the National Maritime Union of America. It had a strong democratic constitution, which included a provision rooting out discrimination. With Joe Curran at its head, the new union encountered many difficulties, especially with communists. But eventually, the organization expanded and built a splendid headquarters building in New York and modern halls in several other port cities. In addition, it enabled its membership to win good wages, better working conditions, and generous pension, health, and welfare benefits.

Becoming an able-bodied seaman in pursuit of a career at sea is a far different experience now than it was earlier in this century. But you, too, might find it satisfying and rewarding work.

MERCHANT MARINE UNLICENSED SAILORS

On a typical merchant ship, sailors make up most of the crew with each worker being assigned to one of the following departments: deck, engine, or steward's.

Deck Department

The entry rating (or grade) in the deck department is that of ordinary seaman who scrubs decks, coils and splices ropes, paints, cleans living quarters, and does other maintenance jobs. He or she may also relieve an able seaman and steer the ship, or act as a lookout to watch for other ships.

Able seamen (often referred to as AB) have a thorough knowledge of every part of the ship and can handle all the gear and deck equipment. Sometimes they act as quartermasters, steer, and serve as lookouts. Some of the skills expected of able seamen include being able to tie common knots, handle mooring lines when the boat is docking or leaving, participate in boat drills, and be familiar with launching lifeboats and life rafts. They must also be familiar with fire prevention and control and do general maintenance work such as is done by ordinary seamen.

The *boatswain* or *bosun* is the highest ranking able seaman. He or she supervises the deck crew, passes on orders from deck officers, and makes certain that these orders are carried out. He or she assists the chief mate, directs the maintenance work, and, when the ship docks, supervises the deck crew.

Engine Department

The entry position here is that of wiper. There are usually from one to three wipers on cargo ships who keep the engine room and machinery clean. Oilers lubricate equipment and may help overhaul and repair machinery. Firers-watertenders check and regulate the amount of water in the boilers, regulate the fuel flow, and check the operation of the condensers and the evaporators that convert salt to fresh water. The electrician repairs and maintains all electrical equipment, and there may also be a refrigeration engineer to make certain all of the refrigerating equipment for perishable cargoes is operating properly.

Steward's Department

The preparation and serving of meals, as well as the cleaning and maintenance of living quarters, are the responsibilities of this department. Beginning jobs like utility hands and mess attendants require no skills. *Utility hands* bring food supplies from storerooms and refrigerators to the kitchen, prepare vegetables, wash cooking utensils, and scour the galley equipment. *Mess attendants* are responsible for setting tables, serving meals, washing the dishes, and cleaning the living quarters. The *chief cook, assistants,* and the *chief steward* must have cooking skills. With the increased use of frozen and prepackaged foods and smaller crews, many ships need fewer personnel in this department.

Working Conditions

Working on a ship can subject you to great temperature extremes. Standing on the deck in the hot sun or during bitter cold windy weather for long periods as a lookout can be as uncomfortable as working in the engine room with its constant high temperature.

Accommodations for sailors are not luxurious, but good meals are served in a mess room, which may double as a recreation hall. On older ships, crews share quarters and have little privacy, but new vessels have single berth rooms. However, even with improved conditions, work on a ship can become boring.

Sailors in the merchant marine work seven days a week, although individuals usually work two four-hour watches or shifts during each twenty-four-hour period, and have eight hours off between each watch. Some sailors are day workers who are on duty eight hours a day from Monday through Friday. When working over forty hours a week, overtime is paid, and when the ship is in port, the basic workweek is forty hours for all crew members.

Job Training

Although not required, a useful background for entering the merchant marine would be previous experience at sea in the Coast Guard or Navy.

A few high schools offer training for marine transportation careers. Perhaps the two outstanding are the Randal Aerospace and Marine Sciences High School in Washington, D.C., and the Food and Maritime Trades High School in New York City, which is located on two World War II ships. Several degree-granting as well as community colleges offer courses. (See *Lovejoy's College Guide* or one of the other guides for available college preparatory courses.) The Harry Lundeberg School, St. Mary's County, Piney Point, Maryland, is perhaps one of the best known professional schools that gives training in entry or beginning job skills as well as advanced courses. Those interested in becoming cooks should obtain information from the Marine Cooks and Stewards Training Program, 350 Fremont Street, San Francisco, CA 94105. The Seamen's Church Institute of New York, 15 State Street, New York, NY 10004, offers a variety of programs in the maritime field.

You can advance in the deck and engine departments by serving for certain periods in a particular job and then successfully passing a Coast Guard examination that tests ability to maintain and use equipment.

Basic Employment Procedures

According to a spokesperson for the National Maritime Union, there are few opportunities in today's merchant marine for the unskilled. It is no longer a job for people who just want to see the world or get away from it all. Those interested have to have more to offer than just physical strength and a desire to work. This is a brief description of how to get a job as an unlicensed (nonofficer) seaman in the U.S. Merchant Marine:

Every person employed aboard an ocean-going U.S. ship must have a Seaman's Certificate, which is issued by the United States Coast Guard. Before it will accept applications for a certificate, the Coast Guard requires that the applicant be referred by a recognized maritime training school or that he or she have a 'letter of commitment' from a shipping company or union addressed to the Coast Guard, stating there is a job available for her or him.

The NMU does not issue such letters of commitment. Most companies also do not issue them except in rare cases. The flow of new seamen required to maintain the normal work force of the U.S. Merchant Marine is achieved mainly through the recruitment of people with certain needed skills or those who have come through maritime training schools or have had training in the armed forces in a skill needed in the merchant marine.

After the Coast Guard issues you a certificate, you register for shipping at the employment office of one of the seamen's unions or at a government agency that employs seamen. Also some oil companies and harbor as well as inland waterways companies do their own hiring. Without previous experience you would be in the lowest seniority group. Qualified seamen in higher seniority groups usually have first claim on available jobs. In the NMU, within each seniority group, the person with the oldest registration card who has the qualifications has the option. A new person, therefore, would have to wait until a job comes down to the lowest seniority group and then must have the oldest card in that group. The job, when it comes, may be for a short trip, relieving the steady person on the job, and then the new seaman would be on the beach again. As he or she achieves higher seniority and higher skills, the waits are likely to become shorter and the jobs steadier.

There is no discrimination by race, creed, color, or sex in NMU and no discrimination on grounds of membership or nonmembership in the union. Applicants can be barred for narcotic offenses or other criminal records and other specific evidence of unsuitability for work at sea. This would be decided jointly by the companies and the union, according to law.

Service in the armed forces is not by itself a factor in determining a new seaman's seniority rating. Service on foreign ships also does not count. Only seatime on American-flag merchant vessels is considered for seniority according to set rules. However, applicants with special skills that the merchant marine needs at the time would be given special consideration by a joint company-union panel.

The period of waiting for a job, once you are registered, depends on how many vessels come into port needing replacements in your category and how many seamen are on the beach waiting for that job. *You must be present in the hall in order to apply for any job.*

For further information about jobs for merchant marine sailors write the Office of Maritime Labor and Training, Maritime Administration, U.S. Department of Transportation, 400 Seventh Street, Washington, DC 20590. Maritime unions also can provide information, and if none are located near you, write to one of those listed in Appendix B.

MERCHANT MARINE OFFICERS

So far we have been describing employment opportunities for seamen who make up the largest group of workers aboard a ship. Those in charge of the vessel are the ship's officers, headed by the captain. The captain has complete responsibility and authority for operating the boat as well as for the safety of the passengers, crew, cargo, and the vessel itself. Serving beneath the captain are officers in the deck and engine departments, as well as a purser, who is a staff officer. The purser handles all the required paperwork, including payrolls, and assists passengers as needed. Some pursers also have been trained as physician's assistants.

To qualify as an officer you must be at least twenty-one, be a United States citizen, obtain a U.S. Public Health Service certificate attesting to your vision, color perception, and general physical condition, and have had at least three years of appropriate sea experience or have graduated from an approved training program. To advance to higher ratings, officers must pass progressively more difficult examinations.

Your best means of becoming a well-trained officer is to attend one of the established training programs such as are available at the U.S. Merchant Marine Academy at Kings Point, New York 11024, which admits students on the same basis as the military academies. You may also want to investigate one or more of the five state maritime academies: California Maritime Academy, Vallejo, CA 94590-0644; Great Lakes Maritime Academy, Traverse City, MI 49684; Maine Maritime Academy, Castine, ME 04421; Massachusetts Maritime Academy, Buzzards Bay, MA 02532; and State University of New York Maritime College, Throgs Neck, NY 10465. Except for the Great Lakes Maritime Academy, which is discussed in a later section, all of these institutions are four-year colleges. A number of trade unions in the maritime industry also provide officer training.

The working hours for officers on board ship are similar to those for seamen. Most officers belong to a maritime union and enjoy excellent pay and living conditions aboard ship.

PORTSIDE JOBS

The merchant marine could not operate without the men and women responsible for loading and unloading the ships at portside. Nor could they operate without those who work in offices doing the necessary planning, recordkeeping, accounting, and purchasing.

In the old days stevedores, or longshoremen, performed all of the manual labor of carrying cargo on and off vessels, but much of that work is now performed by lift trucks and cranes, which cut down the need for manual workers. The introduction of containerization has reduced the employment of longshoremen, too, but there are still opportunities for these workers as the following job titles suggest.

Carloaders load and unload railroad cars, trucks, containers, and barges. Ship cleaners clean the ship's hold, wash painted surfaces, clean and check lifeboats and living quarters, and perform other duties. Marine carpenters crate and pack cargo, repair pallets, and do other work related to wood. Timekeepers keep track of work performed on the docks, ships, barges, and terminals. Billing and manifest clerks do the paperwork while checkers keep track of all goods received or shipped. In addition there is the usual cadre of guards, mechanics, crane operators, ship maintenance personnel, truck drivers, and other workers.

Most ports have an organization called a port authority, which controls activities of the harbor. Many of them have training programs and may be helpful in giving advice about employment. You can obtain a list of such authorities from the American Association of Port Authorities, 1010 Duke Street, Alexandria, VA 22314.

Although many harbor workers learn on the job, clerical and technical skills can be learned in high school or a vocational school. A college degree or previous experience as a ship's officer is helpful when applying for the administrative jobs.

One other area in the portside is the familiar tugboat, which in some harbors is essential for pulling the larger ships into and out of the harbor as well as for towing barges. Here is an opportunity to work on a ship without ever going to sea. The next section discusses tugboats.

INLAND MARITIME CAREERS

Few Americans are aware of the extensive inland waterway system that includes the Great Lakes, the Intracoastal system, and rivers such as the "Mighty Mississippi." Actually about 15 percent of America's total transportation now moves on its inland waters.

Barges carry much of this freight, which consists principally of chemicals, grains, forest products, iron, steel, and petroleum products. These vessels are not manned nor are they self-propelled, but are pulled by a tug or pushed by a towboat.

Here is a world apart from that of the merchant marine. Instead of three departments, each with its set of specialists, most towboats have a crew of two, the captain or master, and the pilot or mate. They work together closely, each standing two six-hour watches per day. If it is a longer route there may be a second mate and they stand two four-hour watches per day, the same as seamen. Those boats that ply the western rivers or the Gulf of Mexico inland waterways need a steersman, who steers the vessel while an engineer is on duty down in the hold of the engine room if it is a larger boat. Towboat cooks are responsible for serving the food they prepare, but deck hands may perform this work on smaller boats.

Responsibilities of the deck hand vary according to the size of the boat and its cargo. Aside from routine duties on the boat, the deck hand ties together the barges to be pulled and later breaks them apart when they reach their port of destination. He or she usually works six hours on, six off, a certain number of days on and off each month, creating a type of schedule and lifestyle that will not appeal to everyone. The work can be dangerous and boring too, but the chance to travel over the waterways has a definite appeal to many.

Another important position is that of the tankerman who loads and unloads liquid cargoes. En route, the tankerman watches the condition of the liquid and checks pumps and engines. He or she may also work in ports, refueling seagoing vessels from bunker barges.

GREAT LAKES MARITIME ACADEMY

One career you may want to explore is that of an officer aboard a ship that serves ports on the Great Lakes. The lake fleet and its personnel are part of the U.S. Merchant Marine, and there is a continuing need for highly trained men and women to operate these ships. The academy explains its program as follows:

This three-year program offers students a variety of academic course work, hands-on experience with state-of-the-art technology and equipment, and over 200 days of "sea time" on board freighters in the Great Lakes. Class sizes are small and instructors are friendly, so you'll receive all the attention you need.

The Maritime Academy offers two career paths. Cadets who choose the "deck" program train to become pilots and mates, navigating ships through open waters and narrow harbors...ships which may stretch to one thousand feet in length and weigh several thousand tons. Graduates may also find satisfying careers in the tug/barge industry.

Cadets who choose the "engine" program train to become the power plant engineers, operating the massive diesel or steam engines that drive these mighty vessels. Like a self-contained floating city, each freighter is supported by complex systems which require highly-skilled attention.

Based on the industry's projected needs for entry-level officers, only about 50 students are admitted to the program each year. There are no age or marital status restrictions. Applicants must be American citizens and have graduated from high school or possess a GED equivalency. Upon graduation, cadets are qualified to write the Coast Guard examinations.

For further information write Great Lakes Maritime Academy, Northwestern Michigan College, 1701 East Front Street, Traverse City, MI 49686.

THE EMPLOYMENT PICTURE

Since the 1980s, employment has dropped significantly because it is directly related to the number of ships on the high seas. Some huge oil tankers have been removed from service and were cut apart for scrap because of the decline in demand for oil. Regulations of the 1990 Oil Pollution Act have doomed many older tank barges and oil tankers. Some newer ships have been constructed, but they were operated by smaller crews because so many of the tasks formerly assigned to seamen have been mechanized. For example, in the older, nonautomated vessels, the engineering department carried twelve sailors. Now there may be only four in newer ships.

The Fleet Size

With Congress attempting to balance the federal budget, subsidies now paid to American shipowners may be reduced or withdrawn. In that case, employment could further decline as ships are withdrawn from service or transferred to foreign registries. The volume of international shipping is not necessarily stable because it depends on the economy of not just the United States, but also its overseas trading partners.

In 1993 the United States had a total of 564 merchant ships of which 367 were privately owned and 197 government owned. Of these 12 were passenger/cargo ships, 321 freighters, 21 bulk carriers, and 210 tankers. Total employment was 9,100. The East Coast wage scale averaged $1,853 a month and the West Coast $2,536, with the monthly wages supplemented with room and board, overtime, and fringe benefits.

Occupational Breakdown

According to the *Occupational Outlook Handbook,* in 1994 there were approximately 48,000 men and women employed in water transportation of whom:

- 45 percent worked on merchant marine ships or U.S. Navy Military Sealift ships;
- 42 percent worked on towboats, tugs, dredges, and other craft in harbors, on canals, on rivers, and on other waterways, as well as piloting boats, and in marine construction, salvaging, and surveying;
- 13 percent worked on passenger-carrying vessels such as sightseeing, cruise, and excursion ships, as well as on ferries.

At the same time the 48,000 jobs represented the occupations shown by the following tabulation:

Seamen and marine oilers	20,000
Captains and pilots	13,000
Engineers	7,600
Mates	7,300

On the whole the job outlook is not expected to improve. Newer ships that enter service require smaller crews, and this increases competition for available positions. Overall employment in water transportation is, therefore, not expected to grow.

OTHER MARINE CAREERS

You do not have to join the merchant marine to find a career in water transportation. Opportunities may lie close to your home if you live on or near the shore. Consider some of the following:

Operation of all-day fishing boats for fishermen who enjoy the sport of deep-sea fishing is a growing business. Boats usually leave early in the morning and return sometime during the late afternoon. Typical advertisements read: "Captain Jones will leave the West Dock daily at

6:00 A.M. for deep-sea fishing ten miles out." Ask the captain of each boat about possible job opportunities. Here you may find good summer or part-time jobs that will give you valuable experience.

In some areas commercial fishing boats depart for distant fishing grounds and remain at sea for several days or weeks as they fill their holds with valuable catches. Even a short-term job on one of these boats can provide experience.

The growth and popularity of private boating has created an expanding marina business. A busy marina is an interesting place to work. Although you may not do much traveling, you will learn how to handle boats and occasionally have a chance to get out on the water. In the north, marinas are a summer business and therefore offer only temporary jobs.

In many parts of the country excursion boats take passengers to distant points of interest or just tour a harbor. They provide jobs for deck hands, engineers, and others in the maritime field, as do ferries. "Moonlight" and "dinner" cruises are popular in many parts of the country for those who enjoy nighttime cruising and eating dinner on shipboard. High school and college students seeking summer employment may find jobs as waiters or waitresses, reservation clerks, cleaners, and in various kitchen positions.

Pick up a Sunday newspaper from a large city and turn to the travel section. You cannot help but be impressed by the number of advertisements for cruises. The era of luxurious trans-Atlantic or trans-Pacific ocean voyages is practically gone, except for the occasional trip, but in their place are luxurious cruises that range all the way from three-day trips to around-the-world voyages. If you study these advertisements you may notice that the ships are of foreign registry, This means that they do not have to observe the stringent American rules that apply to the operation of passenger liners. Furthermore, if they are owned and operated by foreign companies, they are usually staffed by natives of their countries. This may not be true of all the ships that call at a port near you, and certainly not of excursion boats, which offer simple daytime or overnight trips. Since cruise ships are, in reality, floating hotels with every conceivable service for passengers, the list of job opportunities could be long. Your state employment security office may be able to tell you about openings with the cruise lines, and you should also apply directly to the cruise line offices.

Further information about the maritime industry may be obtained by writing the Office of Congressional and Public Affairs, Maritime Administration, U.S. Department of Transportation, Washington, DC 20590. A companion VGM Career Horizons book *Opportunities in Marine and Maritime Careers,* will give you much more detailed information on the subject.

CHAPTER 2

FROM TRAILS TO SUPERHIGHWAYS

We have already seen how thousand of years ago, before roads were constructed, small boats transported goods and people. With the invention of the wheel and the introduction of draft animals, it became possible to reach areas not previously accessible by water and thus open up vast new trading markets. Throughout the ancient world nations constructed fine highways, and as early as 2700 B.C. China had a road system. Around 2000 B.C. Babylon and Ninevah built excellent roads and later a brick road was laid between the two cities. The Egyptian king who erected the Great Pyramid first spent ten years using 100,000 men to build a stone highway so materials could be moved to the pyramid site. However, the world had never seen such a road network as that which connected Rome with all parts of her empire.

The Romans built 50,000 miles of roads to all major European cities so they could reach their conquered lands easily, move troops if necessary, and keep in touch with their armies. The roads were intended to protect the empire, not encourage trade, but since they were so well constructed, it was possible to transport goods over them quickly and economically. Nothing stopped the Roman road builders from using the most direct route. When they came to river, they built a bridge. At a marsh, they filled the bog, and they tunneled through hills that stood in their way. Built to last, messengers on horseback could make a hundred miles a day, and goods could be shipped from England to Rome in thirteen days, going to the coast of Gaul (France) and then by road to the "Eternal City." After the fall of the Roman Empire many roads were neglected, and it was not until the twentieth century that significant road building resumed.

THE EARLIEST AMERICAN ROADS

The first roads on the land that later became the United States were trails found on the midwest plains and in the forests along the Atlantic seaboard. Those out west were paths worn through tall grasses by buffalo and other animals as they chose the easiest routes to reach their feeding grounds, water holes, or nearby streams.

Along the Atlantic seaboard the Indians made their own trails through the forests. Most were eighteen or twenty inches wide and as the braves walked in single file along a narrow trail, they could keep hidden from enemies. This was ample width for a squaw who followed her brave, carrying all their possessions on her back.

Such paths usually followed streams, with necessary crossings being made at shallow pools or across rocks. To ascend a hill the Indian trails wound snakelike through the woods along the side of a slope, which made climbing easier. The early colonists used these trails for roads as they traveled by foot or on horseback from village to village. Gradually woodsmen widened the trails, and they then were referred to as roads.

Where a road began a woodsman made a blaze or ax mark on some of the trees to indicate its type. One ax mark meant it was a *one-chop* road, wide enough for horseback riders. Once the road was broadened so two wagons could pass, two marks were blazed an the trees and it was known as a *two-chop* road. When the ground became smooth enough for coaches, the three ax marks designated it as a *three-chop* road.

Some of the early short roads between New York and Boston, called "post roads," were used by riders who carried mail from town to town. In 1673 mail was dispatched from New York to Boston for the first time. The road was so bumpy, and at times muddy, that few wagons made the trip until 1772, when these primitive highways were considered safe enough for stagecoach travel, although bumpy and at times almost impassible.

That same year a retired Virginia judge, Richard Henderson, eager to sell plots of land in Kentucky, organized the Transylvania Company to buy a large section of the wilderness. He asked his friend, Daniel Boone, to purchase the land from the Cherokee Indians who owned it. Once Boone accomplished this in the spring of 1775, he hired thirty men to help him carve out a roadway from North Carolina through the Cumberland Gap and into Kentucky. When the road builders reached the Kentucky River, they erected a fort and within a short time the new road was crowded with families hurrying west to buy land and build homes. Other roads followed, and soon those pioneers who were eager to leave the East could reach the fertile lands beyond the Alleghenies.

THE TURNPIKE ERA

With the Revolutionary War behind them, many Americans living in the congested cities and suburbs along the Atlantic seaboard hoped to move west to buy land and establish new homes, farms, and businesses. It was a daunting trip, however, for there were few passable wagon roads and fewer inns or taverns to welcome the weary traveler.

The new federal government had no funds to plan, build, or repair roads. Therefore, many wealthy businessmen who had to travel to distant places, were glad to help pay for better roads in their areas. They assisted in establishing companies that would build new highways and charge those who used them. These roads were laid out as straight as the land would permit and wherever possible avoided steep grades or hills. They were called turnpikes because each toll gate had a long pole studded with "pikes" (now called spikes) to close the highway until the traveler paid his toll. Thereupon the pole was swung back so the individual or wagon could pass through. Between 1792 and 1810 it has been estimated that there were 175 private companies in New England operating nearly 3,000 miles of turnpikes.

The first important turnpike was built from Philadelphia to Lancaster, Pennsylvania, in 1791. Instead of the usual narrow winding road, the Lancaster Turnpike Company constructed a highway twenty-four feet wide and paved it with a new type of surface invented by John L. McAdam, a Scottish engineer. It was made of crushed limestone and gravel called *macadam*. Horses and wagons passing over the road crushed the stone and packed it down even more firmly so that when it rained, the water ran off this surface into ditches on either side. For the first time travelers were free from delays caused by mud and ruts.

Other turnpike companies soon opened in the New England and Middle Atlantic states, but by 1825, when the Erie Canal opened, most of them had gone out of business and their stock became worthless because the tolls were insufficient to pay for their maintenance, let alone dividends to the stockholders. This encouraged many entrepreneurs to build canals since turnpikes were not practical, but the canals with their horse-drawn barges and flat-bottom boats were short lived thanks to the new railroads. This left the towns and states to care for the now deteriorating turnpikes and their local roads.

After the Revolutionary War a passable road had existed in Maryland between Baltimore and Cumberland, but that was as far west as one could travel safely. In 1806 President Thomas Jefferson appointed road commissioners to lay out a highway to start at Cumberland and extend to the Mississippi River. Construction began nine years later, and in 1818 the first stagecoach sped down the new highway. People soon referred to it as "Uncle Sam's Pike," "The National Road," or "The Pike," which was misleading since there were no toll gates. By the time it reached the Mississippi River in 1840, railroads were operating in most states and interest in highway construction had dissipated because it was thought that the speedy steam engines provided superior transportation. As a result the states and towns lost interest in maintaining their roads, which led to a period known as "the dark ages of the roads."

The appearance of "horseless carriages" at the turn of the twentieth century sparked a new wave of road building. Those first fragile automobiles had such difficulty coping with the muddy rough roads, that not only flat tires but also breakdowns were frequent. Something had to be done to provide good surface conditions for these new cars coming from several factories.

Cement appeared the best solution, and in 1909, Wayne County, Michigan, laid a mile of cement highway. This sparked the creation of almost 600 "Good Roads" associations dedicated to rebuilding old trails and resurfacing other roads. Wealthy interests organized a company to build the "Lincoln Highway" from Jersey City to San Francisco. Construction began in 1914 and pushed west 3,389 miles, reaching its goal thirteen years later. In 1916 Congress started appropriating money for roads, dividing the funds among the states. At last the goal of "good roads" appeared possible!

PARKWAYS, FREEWAYS, AND INTERSTATES

Just above the line that separates New York City from its northern neighbor, Westchester County, steam shovels were busy digging a new roadway alongside a small muddy stream called the Bronx River. It was 1906 and county officials were taking the first steps to provide good highways for the growing number of automobiles. They had decided to construct a new kind of road—a *parkway*—just for passenger cars.

The county had purchased a narrow fifteen-mile strip of land beside the river. They tore down old buildings, cleared out junk yards, then laid the pavement and planted grass, shrubs, and trees along each side of the road to make a park. The Bronx River Parkway was one of the first "limited access" roads, a highway that motorists could enter or leave at only a few places. Other cities soon built similar parkways, and back in Michigan, Wayne County constructed a new sixteen-mile limited access highway from Detroit to Pontiac. This was not a parkway, however, but a road that went through both business and residential areas and was open to all types of traffic. The trucks proved so noisy and annoying to people living close to the road, that highway planners realized it was not the answer for city traffic.

During the early 1930s, California adopted legislation providing for construction of freeways—limited access roads with no tolls but with trees and grass planted on both sides of the pavement, as well as fencing to prevent people and animals from crossing the roadway. Since that time many miles of wider and wider freeways have been built in California. Down in Texas the state highway department urged all road planners to save trees when widening or straightening roads and also to add plantings to make highways more attractive. At the same time rest stations and picnic areas were constructed.

While Californians were planning freeways and other states were building new highways, Pennsylvania residents suddenly learned that their state was going to build a turnpike, and just as in the days of the Lancaster Turnpike, charge tolls! Because the Lincoln Highway had grades of as much as 9.7 percent (100 feet of road rising 9.7 feet) to get over the Alleghenies, most trucks took a longer route through New York or Maryland.

The Pennsylvania Highway Commission formed a private company to build a new 160-mile express highway across the state. There would be two double lanes of road, one for eastbound and the other for westbound traffic, with tollbooths set up at each exit. There would be no cross roads, red lights, stops, or steep grades, while wide curves would permit traffic to go as fast as ninety miles per hour. The few entrances and exits would be built in the form of cloverleafs for increased safety. Furthermore, by following the right of way of the South Penn Railroad, started after the Civil War but never finished, the railroad bed and its seven half-completed tunnels would save time and money.

The turnpike was completed in twenty months, a record for such construction. Motorists could make better time than the railroad, truckers used it year-round, and at last the historic land barrier between the Atlantic seaboard and the Middle West had been broken.

UNCLE SAM'S SUPERHIGHWAY SYSTEM

The largest public construction project of all time was put into motion in 1944 when Congress passed legislation to provide a National System of Interstate and Defense Highways. It called for 41,000 (since lengthened to more than 45,000) miles of high-speed roads at a cost of $27 billion (also increased considerably). Of every dollar spent Uncle Sam would pay 90 cents and the state 10 cents. Most of the money was to be raised by taxes on gasoline, tires, and auto hardware. When finished the system would link all cities in the United States with populations over 50,000.

As with any project this size, there are bound to be problems, opposition, criticism, and delays. Not all Americans favored superhighways. People in large cities feared the noise, and many did not want to give up scarce open space for a four- or six-lane roadway. In many municipalities and towns, low-income people were displaced when their property was taken for the interstate. Historical neighborhoods were sacrificed, farmers whose land was divided often lost the use of property thus made inaccessible. Parklands, wildlife, and scenic points became threatened, and noise and air pollution were common complaints.

Nevertheless, on the favorable side, superhighways have made life better for many. Interstates have pushed up property values of land lying near them, and adjacent businesses have benefited. Most people agree that as our population keeps growing, more roads are needed as well as more mass transit (buses and trains) to reduce traffic pressure in cities. Even more urgent is the need to maintain properly our huge road system as pavement constantly needs replacing, dangerous cracks and potholes develop, bridges become unsafe, and many curves need to be reduced, to say nothing of the desirability to relocate some roads.

During 1993, the most recent year for which statistics were available as this book went to press, the federal government and the states spent $86,539,000 on highway construction and repairs. All road and highway mileage totaled 3,904,721, of which 45,530 miles were interstate system and the balance laid elsewhere. Despite what the public may think about road conditions, 17 percent of all streets, roads, and highways were judged very good, 19 percent good, 53 percent fair to mediocre, and 11 percent poor.

Although more and larger highways may not be the best answer to today's transportation problems, even in its not quite finished state, our nation's superhighway system, augmented by excellent state, county, and city/town roads, serves us well. Not only do we have the world's finest network of safe highways but also never-ending opportunities for those seeking careers in this vital and exciting nationwide highway construction industry.

CAREER OPPORTUNITIES

As you can see, road and highway construction and maintenance requires a wide range of skilled and unskilled workers. Much of the preparatory work involves material-moving-equipment operators who use different types of machinery to move earth, rock, trees, and other objects that lie in the path of a planned highway. According to the *Occupational Outlook Handbook*: "Excavation and loading machine operators run and tend machinery equipped with scoops, shovels, or buckets to excavate earth at construction sites and to load and move loose materials.

"Grader, dozer, and scraper operators remove, distribute, level, and grade earth with vehicles equipped with blades. In addition to the familiar bulldozers, they operate trench excavators, road graders, and similar equipment. Although many work in the construction industry, grader, dozer, and scraper operators also work for state and local governments mainly in maintenance and repair work."

Almost all jobs in highway construction and maintenance are performed outdoors in sun and rain, heat and cold. In northern climates maintenance may include snowplowing, which is not always a nine-to-five job nor without its discomforts and hazards.

If interested in this type of work, we suggest you visit the nearest office of the state or town highway department. You will find someone who will tell you about job and/or career opportunities with the government as well as local construction companies that have state or town construction or paving contracts. Working during summer vacations as a flag person or manual laborer is a good way to learn the business and get your start. Also contact the nearest state employment security office for information about possible jobs.

For further information contact the American Road and Transportation Builders Association, 501 School Street, SW, Washington, DC 20024.

CHAPTER 3

HAULING FREIGHT BY MOTOR TRUCKS

It might be said that the motor truck industry dates back some 4,000 to 6,000 years ago, when two-wheeled carts and then four-wheeled wagons were first built to carry goods. Pulled by horses, oxen, or other domesticated livestock, animal power was used until the development of the steam engine and then the internal combustion engine around 1900.

Looking back some three hundred years, as already mentioned, Indian trails winding through the forest provided the first roads. Once these were widened to become a one-chop road, a horse and rider or a horse loaded with goods could travel long distances and offer a rudimentary freight service. With the development of two-chop roads, wagons replaced packhorses and larger freight shipments were feasible.

As migrants from the Atlantic seaboard states made their way across the Alleghenies, shippers and businessmen formed wagon trains to transport the goods that new settlers in Pennsylvania, Ohio, and other states were anxious to purchase. The Conestoga wagon was the first efficient freight carrier and led to the introduction of the Prairie Schooner, a covered wagon, used by those crossing the Great Plains. The land was flat, therefore the absence of roads was not a serious deterrent to their passage. Those heading for the west traveled in groups or wagon trains for protection from Indian attacks, as did the supply wagons that serviced isolated military camps and forts.

By 1840–50 most of these trains had disappeared in the east and now wagons were used primarily for short-haul trips or by peddlers who called on customers in remote areas. Trains picked up most of the long-distance freight traffic, and the same transition occurred out west once the transcontinental railroad had opened and other railroads began to crisscross the states.

When automobiles first appeared on city streets around the turn of this century, most trucks were still horse-drawn, except for a few powered by steam or electricity. By 1904 the approximate 700 electric- or gasoline-driven trucks in the entire United States were hardly a threat to the traditional horse and wagon. Solid rubber tires and poor springs ensured such a rough ride for these trucks on the unimproved roads that some goods were easily damaged and long-distance trips were not practical. As is still true today, batteries provided a very short range for the few electrically driven trucks.

World War I gave the trucking industry the impetus it needed as the government awarded numerous contracts for various types of trucks to be used by the army here and abroad. Now that truck operation had become fairly reliable, pneumatic tires had replaced solid rubber, more powerful gasoline engines were available, and more roads were paved, trucks gradually took their place in both short- and long-haul cargo transportation and their number had grown to more than 600,000 by 1918. Finally, some forty-odd years later, the interstate highway system was gradually blanketing the whole nation, and trucks could compete with railroads in earnest.

DISASTER FOR THE NEW HAVEN

As late as the 1950s, huge train yards were busy places in the afternoon. Noisy switch engines put the long freights together so that they would be ready for their scheduled departures in the evening. Some of the faster trains received imaginative names like Red Ball Express, Overland Limited, Merchants Dispatch, or Evening Mercury. Tower workers, conductors, engineers, and dispatchers paid more attention to running these trains on schedule than they did to unprofitable passenger trains. Nevertheless, the future was not bright for the rails. The nation's

40,000-mile interstate highway system had been creeping over mountains, through valleys, and over rivers as it laid mile after mile of smooth four-lane roads and opened exciting new prospects for truckers both large and small.

What happened to the New York, New Haven & Hartford Railroad in New England was typical. Before the New England Thruway (Interstate 95) opened in the late 1950s, numerous fast freights snaked their way along the heavily traveled New York–Boston Atlantic coastline route. Then with the opening of Interstate Highway 95, which enabled trucks to roar between these two cities in four hours, more and more freight was diverted from freight cars to trailer trucks. Lower rates and better service enticed more and more shippers to try the trucks.

Except for heavy shipments of bulk materials such as grain, coal, oil, lumber, livestock, chemicals, and liquefied gas, the railroads were forced to relinquish most of their business to the trucks. Eventually short-haul railroads like the New Haven went into bankruptcy. They then lost their identities altogether as they were forced to merge with other carriers in order to survive.

Freight Categories

There are two kinds of truck freight: *Less Than Truckload* or LTL, and *Truckload.* Less than truckload means a cargo that is insufficient to fill a large truck. Companies that provide LTL service have smaller vehicles that make several stops to pick up enough freight to fill a larger tractor-trailer truck. This truck then carries its cargo to a control terminal where the packages are sorted, and other trucks haul the packages to terminals in various cities. There, they are sorted again and put on smaller trucks for door-to-door delivery.

The second category of freight, truckload, refers to a truck that picks up a complete load of goods from one shipper and hauls it directly to a single company or location in another city. Most of the new companies entering the trucking industry are interested in the truckload business because it is less expensive to operate and may be run with nonunion labor.

THE TRUCKING BUSINESS TODAY

Make no mistake: trucking is a huge business, one of the most important in the transportation field, taking in approximately $110 billion annually. Some forty million trucks are on the roads in the United States and three million in Canada. In 1993 motor trucks hauled 28.7 percent of domestic freight traffic compared to 37.8 percent by railroads, 14.9 percent by inland waterways, 18.7 percent by oil pipelines, and .4 percent by airlines. In the United States the industry employs more than seven million men and women, of whom almost three million are drivers. Since trucking companies are found in almost every part of the United States, there is real employment opportunity for those seeking careers in this business.

Back in 1930, Galen Rousch, an attorney, and his brother, Carroll, founded a small company in Akron, Ohio, which they called Roadway Express. Today the company's headquarters are still in Akron, and it has become the number-one trucker. It grew by buying up smaller companies and then extending its routes throughout the country. With approximately 25,000 tractors, trailers, and trucks, and as many employees, the company takes in over a billion dollars in revenue annually. In a recent year it accepted over twelve million shipments, which it handled in its terminals in more than 400 cities.

The number-one career in trucking is that of driver. Since it offers one of the more glamorous and better paying jobs and does not require specialized formal education, let's first look at what is required to be a long-distance truck driver.

LONG-DISTANCE TRUCK DRIVERS

The powerful headlights of the sixteen-wheel tractor-trailer probed through the thick snowflakes and picked up the road sign pointing to the truck stop. The driver tapped lightly on the brake pedal to release just enough compressed air to slow up the diesel behemoth, its insides crammed with twelve tons of paper. Then the driver expertly turned the wheel to steer the rig into the parking lot across from the combination filling station and restaurant. It is a popular and most welcome spot for truckers driving that lonely road high in the Rockies.

With a slight hissing sound the vehicle stopped. After checking the brakes, parking lights, and instrument panel, the driver opened the door, jumped down to the white pavement and ran over to the building.

"Well, look who's here," the counterman called as the snow-covered figure slammed the door and stamped on the doormat. "You're ten minutes behind your usual schedule. Not going to let a little storm slow you up, are you?" he teased.

"You should see it up there," the other replied and pointed up the road. "Just barely missed two trucks that had jackknifed this side of the pass. Couldn't stop my rig on that slick. Called for help on my CB. I'm lucky I made it down the grade without skidding off the road."

The woman shrugged out of her coat, shook it, and then brushed the snow off her hair. "My children should see me tonight," she observed. "They think their mom has a cinch of a job sitting up in that truck cab, wheeling down the highway at sixty. So does my husband, for that matter!"

Joan Doran is one of the many women who drive large long-distance trucks today. They drive because they need to earn money, they enjoy the freedom of the open road, and they like the responsibility of driving a $100,000 machine loaded with expensive cargo.

Joan is one of the growing number of women truckers. Most truckers live near large cities and manufacturing centers where there are many truck terminals. On the other hand, some drivers specialize in transporting such goods as minerals or agricultural products and live in rural areas.

A good proportion of these long-distance truck drivers work for companies that offer services to businesses in general. Some are employees of specialized companies, such as furniture manufacturers that own and operate their own trucks. A number of drivers also own their own trucks and either operate independently, serving a number of businesses, or work under a lease arrangement to a trucking company.

Note should also be made of the industrial truck operators who drive small electric-powered trucks and forklifts within industrial plants. Their vehicles haul heavy machinery, motors, parts, and other materials to and from all locations in a factory or industrial complex.

Employment Outlook

The job outlook for long-distance drivers is good. The number of jobs in this field is expected to grow about as fast as the average for all occupations through the year 2005. If the nation's economic growth lives up to economists' projections, there will be a corresponding growth in the amount of freight carried by truck over long distances, thus increasing the demand for drivers.

Still, we should point out some interesting factors that might affect the job market for long-distance drivers. Larger trucks will increase the amount of freight each driver can haul, thus cutting down somewhat the number of trucks needed. At the same time, however, some experienced drivers will transfer to other work, retire, or die, creating many openings for new drivers. Nevertheless, since earnings are high and little training is required, there will be stiff competition for every job opening.

Wages, Hours, and Unions

As with other forms of transportation, job opportunities vary from year to year as freight volume increases or decreases. In good times, many new drivers are hired; in times of recession, some drivers are laid off and others may work fewer hours.

Drivers who work for large trucking companies usually enjoy the highest wages. Rates of pay are fairly uniform because this occupation is highly unionized. Union contracts are often master agreements covering all employers within a multistate region. Earnings of each driver will vary, though, depending on the number of miles he or she drives, the number of hours worked, and the type of truck driven.

In addition to the vehicles operated by the large, long-distance companies, there are firms such as dairies and bakeries that own their own fleets and pay their drivers on the same basis as their other employees. Usually the wage is for a specified number of hours, and if the drivers work additional hours, they are paid overtime. A workweek of at least fifty hours is not uncommon. These drivers sometimes belong to the unions that represent the other plant employees, whereas most men and women who are long-distance drivers are members of the International Brotherhood of Teamsters.

Qualifications and Training

Minimum qualifications for long-distance truck drivers who are engaged in interstate commerce are set by the Department of Transportation. You must be at least twenty-one years old, pass a physical examination, and have good hearing, 20/40 vision with or without glasses, the normal use of arms and legs, and normal blood pressure.

Some trucking companies have additional hiring standards. Many have a minimum age of twenty-five; others specify height and weight limitations. Some require applicants to have had several years experience driving trucks long distances. All employers seek men and women with good driving records who can pass a road test operating the type of truck that will be driven in regular service. In addition, they must take a written examination on the Motor Carrier Safety Regulations of the U.S. Department of Transportation, and in most states truck drivers must have a chauffeur's license or commercial driving permit.

A high school driver-training course is good background, and a high school course in automotive mechanics is also helpful inasmuch as it will enable you to make minor roadside repairs. Some technical-vocational schools offer truck driving courses. But before taking such a course, check with prospective employers to make certain that the school's training is acceptable. A more common method of entering a truck driving career is to start as a dockworker and advance from this position to driving a small panel truck and then perhaps a larger truck in local service.

Newly hired drivers are taught how to prepare the forms used on the job, receive a small amount of driving instruction, and practice on a training course to learn how to maneuver the larger trucks. Then they will make one or more training trips under the supervision of an instructor or experienced driver.

Opportunities for promotion are limited, generally only to positions as safety supervisor, driver supervisor, or dispatcher. Most drivers are not interested in these jobs, however, because the starting pay usually is less than what they earn in driving positions.

For further information about career opportunities in long-distance trucking, write the American Trucking Association, 2200 Mill Road, Alexandria, VA 22314.

You should know that the trucking industry established a nonprofit organization, The Professional Truck Driver Institute of America. It certifies truck-driver training programs that meet industry standards and will send you a free list of certified tractor-trailer driver training programs. Their address is 8788 Elk Grove Boulevard, Elk Grove, CA 95624.

LOCAL TRUCK DRIVERS

Local trucks, which operate within a city, town, or limited area, usually do the initial pickups from plants and factories and take freight to terminals where it may be consolidated with other shipments or placed directly on a long-distance truck. These same local trucks may pick up freight that has arrived at the terminal, and then deliver it to stores and homes.

Local truck drivers must be skilled and able to maneuver their vehicles through dense traffic and into tight parking spaces, thread their way through narrow alleys, and expertly back up to loading platforms.

The trucking industry is so diversified that it is impossible to mention all the types of companies that offer career possibilities. If this business interests you, obtain a chauffeur's license and start your job search right at home by considering some of the businesses that operate their own trucks.

Some of these businesses employ drivers who are combination salespeople and drivers, as in many laundry, dry cleaning, milk, and bakery businesses. Don't overlook the possibilities of a career as a driver with a fuel oil supplier who sells gasoline, bottled gas, and heating oil. A lumber yard that makes deliveries of building supplies, a road construction company that operates a fleet of trucks and other heavy equipment, a bulk milk company that delivers milk in huge stainless steel containers, and the small retail stores that operate one or more delivery trucks all could offer employment opportunities.

OPPORTUNITIES FOR NONDRIVERS

Not everyone wants to be a truck driver, nor can everyone qualify for the position. There are many other job opportunities in the trucking industry. We have already noted that Roadway Express employed upwards of 19,000 employees, and the next largest company, Consolidated Freightways, had more than 18,000 employees. These are but two of several large trucking firms, all of which need a variety of skills to operate their far-flung businesses successfully.

The truck on the road is like the tip of the iceberg. To keep the trucks filled and running every day calls for a huge, nationwide organization. The latest in management methods, computer technology, communication equipment, and automotive maintenance keep the company going and the trucks moving.

Take Consolidated Freightways, for example. There, when a customer telephones an order for a shipment to be picked up, he or she sets in motion a highly efficient system. A trained employee takes down the details, and the minute the customer hangs up, the order is telephoned by radio to the nearest radio-controlled truck so that the driver can swing by the plant and make the pickup. As soon as the freight is loaded on the truck, the driver gives the customer a "pro" or identifying number. Later, if he or she should have any questions about the shipment, the information can be retrieved instantly from the computer by using this number.

While the truck is on its way to make the pickup, the pricing is being done by the computer. All the necessary paperwork, such as writing up a bill of lading and preparing the manifest, are also being done electronically.

The location of the truck with the recent pickup and the location of every other truck the company is operating appear on a huge map of the United States in a control center. This system enables employees to monitor every vehicle continuously and pinpoint just where any shipment is in a matter of seconds. Thanks to long-line telephone communications, all company operations are coordinated throughout the country.

As for customer relations, hundreds of representatives contact shippers and are available to help answer questions, solve problems, or assist in planning and shipping programs.

Imagine the fascination of working as a member of such a team in some clerical capacity, as an accountant, or a computer, communications, or management specialist.

When surveying the trucking industry, let's not forget those hundreds of truck terminals, airfreight depots, and special sales offices, each staffed with personnel who handle all the clerical functions. Let's also remember the dock personnel who load and unload the trucks and sort freight, as well as the mechanics and others who service and repair the vehicles. Here is an essential business that uses workers with many skills to keep freight moving twenty-four hours a day, seven days a week.

Although the large trucking companies move much of the nation's heavy freight, there is another nationwide company that specializes in transporting only small packages, none weighing more than 150 pounds. It is probably the best known trucker in the United States.

THE FLEET OF BROWN TRUCKS

Sitting behind a desk that had once been a lunch counter, the young man was busy answering the two old-fashioned telephones that rang from time to time. His new undertaking, the American Messenger Company, consisted of the phones, two bicycles, six messengers, and himself, James Casey. It was 1907 and his basement office was located in downtown Seattle.

The messengers had to be courteous and neat to impress Mr. Casey and qualify for a job. They delivered papers and articles for local businesses and individuals in the Seattle area. Occasionally they were called upon to walk dogs or to carry an elderly woman's groceries.

Business was not brisk, but gradually the tiny enterprise grew. Casey changed the name to Merchants Parcel Delivery in 1913. At the same time he bought his first horseless carriage, a Model-T Ford. A year later seven motorcycles were added, and soon Merchants was handling all the deliveries for three of the largest department stores in the Seattle area.

In 1919 the company opened an office in Oakland and changed its named to United Parcel Service, at the same time adopting the official UPS color, brown. Other "firsts" followed, such as the first brown uniforms for drivers, the first substation in Long Beach, and the first conveyor belt, which was 180 feet long. It made handling packages more efficient.

The employee magazine, the *Big Idea,* appeared in Los Angeles in 1924. In its first issue Jim Casey wrote: "Here's to the success of the *Big Idea,* as a means of fostering a spirit of friendship, cooperation, and goodwill among all of us who are brought together by UPS. The business has grown to the size where it is no longer possible for all of us to know each other so intimately as would naturally be the case. But, it is intended that this shall always be a human organization. I want all to know some of the purposes, policies, and ideas of this company to the end that the greater possible good may come to customers and employees alike." Today each UPS district has its own local *Big Idea,* which includes twelve to sixteen pages of company-wide news.

It seemed that nothing could stop the growth of this dynamic company. UPS service was extended to every major West Coast city. Then the first brown trucks started rolling on New York City streets on July 14, 1930, and by year-end the fleet was delivering all parcels for 123 stores. Soon people in Midwestern states were seeing the brown trucks, and today every state except Alaska is served by the company.

In 1953 the management decided to offer UPS service not only to businesses but to anyone who wanted to ship a parcel. By 1996 UPS employed some 335,000 men and women, operated thousands of delivery and feeder vehicles, maintained a fleet of its own airplanes, and had hundreds of buildings spread across the nation. These buildings house highly specialized sorting devices.

The secret of UPS's success is consolidating packages at every point from pickup to delivery. This system enables the company to deliver the maximum number of packages in the minimum amount of time and number of miles. The small package shipments are fed into one highly specialized system. That system starts in the package car as the driver delivers packages and at the same time picks up those articles ready for shipment.

All these packages are then consolidated at the nearest center with those picked up by other drivers. Tractor-trailer units feed the packages from surrounding centers into a hub facility each night. Here they are all sorted and loaded into outgoing feeder vehicles that will take them to the UPS facility closest to their destination. Thanks to a highly mechanized sorting system, a hub like that at Montgomery, Alabama, can handle about 34,000 packages each night in less than four hours.

An equal amount of attention is given to the loading of each delivery truck. By the time each driver arrives for work he or she finds that other workers have loaded the truck in the proper sequence so that deliveries can be made as quickly as possible over the most direct route.

No matter how remote the address of either the shipper or receiver, UPS pickup and delivery service is available, and each package is delivered directly to the door of the consignee. In addition, the company maintains customer counters at each of the operating locations. Here individuals and business shippers can bring their packages rather than have them picked up.

As you may well imagine, this nationwide service depends on people: the men and women who answer the telephones and take your orders for pickups; the drivers who deliver and pick up the packages; the sorters at the various facilities; the drivers of the huge tractors and trailers that carry the packages long distances between centers and hubs; the maintenance people who keep the trucks clean and in top operating condition; the various clerical people in the offices; and the supervisory and administrative staff—all help keep UPS going.

UPS is such an efficient company that it standardizes and codes all of its operations. If you have a flat tire, you have a *471*; if you need road service, you call for a *388*. Neatness is still high on the list of personnel "musts." Trucks, too, must be clean and to keep them that way, they are washed every night.

By 1996 the United Parcel Service had become the world's largest package distribution company, handling a million packages daily at over a thousand distribution sites including forty-nine international locations—

truly a global organizations! It also operated one of the world's largest fleets of airplanes from its airline headquarters in Louisville, Kentucky. In 1996 the airline division was working on long-range plans to convert its Boeing 727 cargo planes to passenger configurations each weekend to fly charter operations Saturdays and Sundays when the planes are normally idle.

A word of caution for those interested in working for UPS either as drivers or sorters and loaders in distribution centers. The company's injury rate in 1995 was slightly higher than the national average for transportation companies. If you do not believe you can safely handle heavy packages, think twice before applying for jobs that require this activity. For information about employment, ask a UPS driver where you may apply locally.

Mention should be made of the fast-growing and successful Federal Express Company, which also delivers correspondence and small shipments anywhere in the country overnight, using its own fleet of aircraft. Roadway Express and several other companies are obtaining market niches, making this a growing and increasingly prosperous industry.

THE LOCAL AND LONG-DISTANCE MOVERS

Another large segment of the trucking industry is devoted to moving. These companies transport furniture, pianos, and other household goods.

Back in 1891 two brothers living in Sioux City, Iowa, decided to earn their fame and fortune. They obtained a large cart, a strong horse, and lettered the side of the wagon: "Bekins, Moving & Storage." John and Martin Bekins had very little money, but lots of ambition and a sincere interest in each customer's individual needs.

One hundred years later, Bekins had grown to become the largest moving and storage company in the world, with over 400 locations in the United States and operations in more than 100 foreign countries. The company claimed that the brothers original spirit was sustained and that personal service was still the cornerstone of the business, even though the company handles more than 900 moves each day.

This may seem like an astronomical number of moves for just one company, but perhaps it is not so surprising when you consider that about 40 million Americans, or a fifth of the population, move each year. It is the moving and storage industry that makes it possible for families to pack up and make moves of hundreds or thousands of miles, with every detail surrounding the move anticipated and efficiently handled.

Furniture movers employed by interstate companies often work in crews of three or four, one of whom is the driver who also loads and unloads along with the other movers. If one of the helpers is qualified to drive the truck, it may be possible for the van to make an uninterrupted long-distance trip. Such movers may be away from home for weeks at a time. They lead irregular lives with sixty hours of work being considered a normal workweek.

Ability to read, write, and do arithmetic; a strong back; good coordination; a sense of responsibility; and a willingness to be helpful and courteous are the main personal requirements for this job. Drivers must hold a Class I driver's license for the kind of equipment they will be driving. Many companies give their employees training in both packing and driving.

The majority of furniture movers work for local companies that do short-haul or local moving and also act as agents for interstate and international movers. The large moving companies have their own movers who may travel throughout the country as they transport several loads before returning to their regular terminal.

As the population continues to grow and people keep changing homes, the demand for movers should increase somewhat. Promotion to the position of estimator is possible for a mover. This person determines the weight and cost of shipping a houseful of furniture. A mover with a thorough knowledge of the business might be considered for promotion to dispatcher. The dispatcher is responsible for routing all the trucks and keeping in touch with all the drivers.

In addition to the usual clerical positions, there are openings for billing clerks, claims adjusters, maintenance workers, mechanics, and administrative personnel.

A word of warning: the moving business is a seasonal one. The busiest time is during the summer months of June, July, August, and September when children are not in school. The last week of each month is usually the busiest time.

For the names and addresses of prospective employers, look in the yellow pages of your telephone book under "Movers." For further information write American Trucking Associations, 2200 Mill Road, Alexandria, VA 22314.

Because trucking is vital to American industry, a career in this sector of transportation is well worth considering. Although much of America's freight moves long-distance by air and rail, remember that in most instances the shipments must reach the plane or freight car by truck. At their destination they must be trucked again.

CHAPTER 4

EVOLUTION OF MASS TRANSIT

Imagine for a moment you are waiting on the corner for a bus to take you to school or work. It is snowing and you stamp your feet to keep from freezing. At last the bus comes, the door opens, and you can feel the welcome warmth. Seconds later you settle back in a comfortable seat and relax. Now go back in time. It is 1716 when you are aboard an open wagon with only a cloth or wooden roof for protection from the elements. You are one of twelve passengers sitting on four benches (without backs). From time to time your seatmates try to brush the new-fallen snow from their clothes, the more fortunate ones huddling beneath bearskins with their protective fur. The horses plod along at four miles an hour on the snowy roadway, making the 170-mile trip an endless nightmare, broken only by infrequent stops at stages (rest stations) along the way.

More comfortable enclosed stagecoaches with crude strap springs, usually pictured in history books, did not appear until later. Although their ride was jolting and jarring, at least they offered protection from bad weather for the fortunate passengers riding inside.

Shortly before the Boston to Newport service began, the first predecessor of today's mass transit commenced service when a six-passenger hackney coach offered short rides within New York City's Bowery. By 1830 large vehicles called *omnibuses* (from the Latin "for all") made their way up and down Manhattan. Some twenty years later rails were laid in the streets and "horsecars" resembling railroad coaches pulled by horses, replaced the lumbering omnibuses. The resulting ride was much smoother, faster, and easier for the horses.

As early as 1873 cable cars were introduced in several cities using steam engines to power the underground cable apparatus. However, these were expensive to build and several inventors were working to perfect motors large enough to propel cars by using electric power from overhead or underground wires. In 1888 Frank J. Sprague successfully operated trolleys in Richmond, Virginia, and showed they were both economical to run and strong enough to carry a full load of passengers even up grades. Within twenty years many cities had elaborate street car systems, and by 1915 trolleys were running over 45,000 miles of tracks.

Subsequently trolley service expanded from downtown metropolitan areas out to rural areas later called suburbs. This enabled cities to expand as the first housing projects started rising near the newly laid tracks.

PUBLIC TRANSIT

At the turn of the century it was possible to travel all the way between New York and Boston by electric trolley, if you had the time and the patience to make the innumerable changes required. What is more, it was said that one might go most of the way from New York to Chicago via local trolleys and interurban lines. It was a time when trolley fever gripped the whole country and even small towns laid single track lines with turnouts every so often to permit the cars to pass.

Trolleys took commuters to work, housewives to market, the wealthy to the opera, children to school, and vacationers to amusement parks or sparkling lakes. As long as there were passengers to fill the seats of the swaying cars this was a relatively inexpensive, safe, and dependable way to travel.

Webster's dictionary defines transit as "local transportation especially of people by public conveyance." Our story starts when the trolley era gave way to the automobile and then the bus.

Once the public had discovered the convenience of owning an automobile, many people gradually abandoned the trolley, especially in small towns. Later, the development of bigger buses for use in cities and large towns provided greater convenience and safety for passengers. They could board or leave the vehicles at the curb rather than in the middle of the street where trolley tracks had to be. Then "Trackless Trolleys" were developed to give the trolley cars greater flexibility, but the cars still had to draw current from overhead wires that were supported by unsightly poles.

As cities grew, trolleys were unable to handle the growing number of passengers traveling into and within urban areas. Subways were dug to supplement the surface transportation. Today, although trolleys have disappeared altogether from New York and many other cities, you can ride one in Boston where they are still used, along with buses and subway trains within a coordinated transit system.

Elsewhere America's most unusual trolley cars are undoubtedly San Francisco's, which are as much a part of that city as the steep hills for which their endless cables and quaint cars were constructed. The cars are not the most efficient form of transportation but they are invaluable as a tourist attraction for the city.

LIGHT RAIL TRANSIT

The trolley is not entirely a thing of the past, however. It is making a comeback in a slightly different form from earlier versions. One of the first new lines, the "Tijuana Trolley," opened in July 1981. It glides down sixteen miles of abandoned track and right-of-way between San Diego, California, and the Mexican border.

Fourteen electric trolley cars were expected to carry 10,000 riders a day as they made their eighteen stops along the way, but management was amazed when some 11,500 passengers clamored to board the cars. Soon their number grew to 18,000. The line proved so successful that another seventeen-mile trolley line was planned for the benefit of residents living in San Diego's eastern suburbs.

Far to the east, in Buffalo, a 6.4-mile light rail system with fourteen stations pushed out from downtown to the State University of New York campus, the first part of an ambitious multiphase plan.

Meanwhile Los Angeles was working on a design to build a midtown elevated railroad, an overhead electric "people mover." Similar lines were being projected in Detroit and Miami. Enormously expensive to build, 80 percent of the cost would be paid for by the Urban Mass Transportation Agency, which is concerned with helping cities solve their transportation problems. However, by 1996 no governmental grants were forthcoming.

Subways are not a thing of the past either. In the 1960s, San Francisco built its extensive Bay Area Rapid Transit (BART) system. Altanta opened the first 7.1 miles of its projected 53-mile MARTA system in September 1979. But the most ambitious new subway opened its first 4.6 miles of track on March 29, 1976, when the Washington Metropolitan Area Transit Authority dispatched its first train on what would eventually be a 98-mile system. Here, as in San Diego, the public's response exceeded all expectations. Some 21,000 passengers were boarding at the five stations of the planned eighty-six-station system; 21,000 men, women, and children, compared to the anticipated 8,000!

Subways provide only part of essential transport services because surface transportation is equally vital to the needs of travelers within an urban area. As already mentioned, most of the urban and suburban transport service is provided by buses. Yet we should not overlook the trolleys, subways, and light rail trains that are also important to any transit system. The light rail trains operate principally in a limited-stop service, such as is offered in San Diego or Buffalo.

The introduction of computers and other automatic devices by the newer transit systems is making these organizations most interesting places to work. A brief look at the new Washington Metro system will suggest a few of the innovations that are making some transit careers so intriguing.

WASHINGTON METRO

The Washington Metro was established in 1966 to plan, construct, finance, and provide for the operation of a rapid rail and bus transit system for the Washington metropolitan area. It was to be managed by elected officials from the District of Columbia, Maryland, and Virginia.

From the very beginning, it was decided that the bus and rail systems would complement, not compete with, each other. Buses would take riders into outlying Metro stations.

As the rail system continues to expand, the bus routes are coordinated with it. The local governments whose representatives manage the Metro set the level of bus service in their areas, where and how often the buses run, thus determining how much or how little they want to provide their taxpayers.

Metrobus

The Metrobus system, which operates a fleet of approximately 1,800 buses, complements the rail service with its 400 basic bus routes and some 800 route variations, making it the fourth largest bus system in the country. All of the buses are equipped with two-way radios, silent radio alarms, flashing lights for protection, and air-conditioning for comfort.

In the communications center, radio dispatchers are constantly on duty providing two-way communication with each Metrobus operating in the region. This enables the dispatcher to adjust quickly to any unexpected crisis, such as an accident. A silent alarm built into the radio system enables police to respond to an operator's signal for help.

The system has modern bus garages for the storage, maintenance, and repair of its vehicles. Most of these are located in the outer suburbs to give more efficient service to Maryland and Virginia passengers, since many of the bus lines act as feeders into the Metro trains.

Metro Trains

This is how the Metro described its automatic train system:

People, backed up by highly sophisticated communications and control equipment, run Metro.

Safety, efficiency, and security were prime considerations in the selections of an advanced wayside control system, computer-assisted control center, radio communication, a 2,000-line capacity private telephone network, system-wide public address systems, TV surveillance network, and a failsafe system for nearly every conceivable equipment malfunction or human error.

Although trains operate automatically in normal service, a well-trained operator sits at the control console, opens and closes doors, announces upcoming stations, communicates with central control, informs passengers of items that may affect their trip, takes manual control of the train at a moment's notice, and performs scores of other duties.

He [or she] takes orders from the supervisors in central control, but, like the captain of a ship, bears first-line responsibility for the well-being of the passengers, which may number more than 1,500 on an eight-car train during peak periods.

Here is a description of the control room:

Control room supervisors, having an electronic overview of the entire Metro system, make and implement decisions to keep it running smoothly.

The operations control center, located in the Metro headquarters building, is the hub of the vast Metro communications and control network.

Control room supervisors perform three major tasks: taking corrective action as problems occur, dispatching repair crews for equipment malfunctions or failures, and performing emergency communications.

When trains fail to move as they should, the supervisors choose and execute a solution after considering a list of options. When a malfunction occurs, the supervisors know whom to call to fix it. In an emergency, the supervisor summons help via police and fire hot lines.

Train control supervisors operate two push-button consoles, one for train operations and the other for Metro support systems. Eight CRT (TV) screens arranged in two horizontal rows face the consoles. The supervisor at the train operations console monitors and controls train movement. The supervisor at the other console handles problems with support systems, such as the electrical substations, station air-conditioning, tunnel ventilation, drainage, station fire and intrusion alarms, and other facilities.

Support system failures appear as alarms on the CRT screens, or they are called in by station attendants.

The train operations supervisor uses the CRT screens as electronic windows to view schematic representations of tracks, trains, and stations throughout the Metro system. Displays on the screen show tracks, cross-overs, turnouts, pocket tracks, stations, and moving trains. As the train (shown in triangles moving along the track lines) enters the station (shown as open rectangles), the rectangles are filled in to show that the train in the station has its doors open.

If a train falls behind schedule by more than a minute, an alarm flashes on the screen showing the time when the train fell behind. By asking the computers via the console, the supervisor learns the complete history of the train's movement for the last five stations, enabling him [or her] to find the cause of the current delay. He [or she] may keep hands-off and allow the computer to correct the delay, which is one of its programmed functions. He [or she] may also execute a plan in which some of the trains ahead and some behind the slow train will mimic its movements in sequence, thus maintaining constant spacing.

All transit systems are not as automated as Washington's, but many of the newer ones have incorporated numerous electronic and fail-safe systems to protect their passengers. Even the older systems like those in Boston, Chicago, and New York are gradually adopting many of these innovations, but it is difficult and expensive to modernize these older subway and bus operations.

TRANSIT TECH

If a transit career interests you, inquire about possible transit tech courses in your local vocational/technical schools. In 1986 "Transit Tech" was instituted in New York City and 400 students applied to the High School of Transit Technology. In 1995, 5,000 students filed applications to study both underground and surface train mechanics.

A retired subway car provides real laboratory experience for the student body, 25 percent of whom are female. Welding, rail car maintenance, climate control (air-conditioning), and electronics are a few of the courses offered. With over sixty cities expecting to expand or develop transit systems, the demand for transit workers is expected to grow and offer good careers in mass transit.

EMPLOYMENT

In the transit sector of transportation the greatest number of jobs is for bus drivers. In fact in 1994 there were approximately 140,000 bus drivers employed mostly in large cities. The majority of them worked for transit lines. Another 425,000 drove school buses, and a few others were employed by churches, commercial interests, and sightseeing companies, 40 percent of whom worked part time.

Driving Occupations

Most experienced drivers have regularly scheduled runs, but new drivers are usually placed on an "extra" list to substitute for regular drivers who are ill or on vacation. They may also be assigned to extra and special runs, for example during morning or evening rush hours, or to stadiums when there are special sporting events. In some cities or towns, transit buses transport school children to and from school and extra-list drivers may operate these buses. New drivers remain on the extra list until they have enough seniority to get a regular run, which may take several years.

Promotional opportunities are limited, but experienced drivers can rise to jobs as dispatchers or supervisors and eventually to management positions. Dispatchers assign buses to drivers, make sure drivers are on schedule, reroute buses when necessary, and dispatch extra buses and drivers whenever there is an accident or breakdown and additional vehicles are needed.

To apply for a position as a bus driver you should be at least twenty-one years old, be in good health, have good eyesight with or without glasses, and have a good driving record. A number of employers prefer applicants who have a high school education or its equivalent. The majority require applicants to pass a physical examination and a written test showing they can follow complex bus schedules. Most states require bus drivers to have a chauffeur's license, which is a commercial driving permit. Drivers face many minor annoyances, such as difficult passengers, traffic tie-ups, bad weather, and fatigue. A relaxed personality is important for this work.

Operators of trolleys and subway trains will find that most of the above qualifications apply to them as well, but specific requirements will vary from city to city. Training is received on the job as is the case with engineers on railroads, and in some systems it may take years before you will be on a regular run.

Note: If you apply for a position with a publicly owned bus or transit system—and most of them are—you will find that all of the jobs are under civil service. This means that appointment to a position, and later promotion, may depend on your taking a competitive civil service examination.

Other Transit Jobs

Next to driving occupations, probably the most number of jobs will be found in the maintenance and repair shops of buses, trolleys, and subways. All vehicles must be kept in top running condition, and since most of them are used practically every day they must get frequent checks and maintenance. They are also taken out of service periodically for major repairs. All this work is usually performed by employees of the transit companies.

Cleaners, mechanics, electricians, welders, painters, upholsterers, and glaziers are some of the specialists needed to keep a fleet of transit buses and trains moving. The best way to prepare for such openings is to take special training at a trade school.

In most cities, transit service operates late into the evening or all night, as is the case in New York City. As a new worker, you will probably be assigned to the night or late shift. As you get seniority, you will be able to bid for better and perhaps more regular working hours.

In the office of any transit company you will find the usual clerical, computer, and receptionist positions. In addition, there are those posts that call for specialized or college training. You will find such positions in the sales, purchasing, public relations, planning, finance, and budget departments. Although turnover in these administrative offices is not likely to be high, investigate the opportunities anyway.

Advantages and Disadvantages

Here are some reasons why you should enter this field, if it interests you:

1. Most jobs are open to everyone because they are under your local municipal or other civil service system. This means that all people, including minorities, are guaranteed equal consideration for positions.
2. There are good chances for promotion because many of these systems are large. Those who have college degrees and/or many years of experience may be in line for promotion to supervisory and managerial posts.
3. Benefits are greater than in many other fields. The overtime, pensions, sick leave, health care, and paid vacations are more generous than in most industries.
4. There is better than average job security, especially after you have been on the job several years.

On the other hand every job has its drawbacks and you should be prepared to face these possible disadvantages:

1. Your income will rise slowly from year to year because every job is paid according to an established salary scale,
2. You may work under great pressure and difficult conditions especially when accidents, breakdowns, storms, or other problems cause the whole system to slow down or cease operating altogether.
3. Public transportation operates seven days a week in most places and in some cities around-the-clock. Therefore you can expect that the chances are good you will have to work shifts.
4. Being a public transportation employee or "public servant" can subject you to unpopularity since many people think that transport workers do not work hard enough, are paid too much, and receive too many benefits.

During a recent year, 80 percent of commuters' trips to the central business districts of Chicago and New York City were made by public transit. In Philadelphia it was 64 percent and 50 percent in Cleveland

and Seattle. It can be seen, therefore, that transit provides transportation services that are essential to the economic well-being of every urban area.

For further information about job openings, contact your state employment security office, the public transit authority, or the municipal civil service office. If you need additional information, write the American Public Transit Association, 1201 New York Avenue, NW, Washington, DC 20005.

TROLLEY AND TRAIN MUSEUMS

On April 19, 1939, the derailing of a trolley on a fan trip over the former Androscoggen and Kennebec Street Railway in Lewiston, Maine, inspired three young men to found the Seashore Trolley Museum in Kennebunkport, Maine, two months later. This was the beginning of a worldwide movement to establish and preserve operating street railway museums. Street railroads were disappearing quickly as buses took their place, and by the end of World War II several museums, both trolley and rail, had been established to acquire cars that otherwise would be discarded and possibly torched.

If you are a trolley or rail fan interested in a volunteer position in one of the many transportation museums that opened around the country, see the annual "Guide to Recreational Railways" in the May issue of *Trains*. Some of the museums offer limited full-time employment also.

THE INTERCITY PEOPLE MOVERS

Recently when a large Concord Coach bus left Littleton, New Hampshire, bound for Colbrook, New Hampshire, sixty miles north, one passenger was aboard. Since this was not unusual, the company dropped the run, leaving all the residents of the North Country between Littleton and Canada without any bus or train service.

In November, 1982, the Bus Regulatory Reform Act went into effect making it easy for carriers to drop unprofitable runs, acquire new routes, and set their own fares and schedules without government approval. Since then the larger companies have been cutting service on many routes because former riders were now driving their own cars or taking airplanes, and this had reduced their fares. During the first two years after deregulation went into effect, some 3,700 communities lost all their bus service. This meant that most of the citizens of these communities no longer had any public surface transportation.

"The magnitude of the impact on some of these towns and some of the people cannot be expressed," Steven Menaugh, of the Kansas Corporation Commission, observed.

The picture is not all bad, however. When Robert Else, III, took over his father's bus company, King Coal Trailways, which was headquartered in Mount Carmel, Pennsylvania, it was a tiny line, operating one passenger bus and carrying no more than 5,000 people for the year. Five years later a fleet of thirteen passenger buses transported some 53,000 passengers annually. Thus King Coal Trailways was a good example of how a small businessman could start a local bus line and serve an area that large companies could not afford to include on their long-distance routes. Since 1982 more than a thousand operators have gone into business, bringing new service to many rural areas that otherwise would never see a bus speed along their roads.

Since buses still play an important part in our overall transportation system, it would be interesting to note how Greyhound started from a one-vehicle, short-haul operation and grew into the largest intercity bus carrier in the world. To do this, let's turn back the calendar to the year 1912.

THE GREYHOUND LINES

If you have a good atlas, you will find the mining town of Hibbing, Minnesota, in the northeastern part of the state. Hibbing's chief claim to fame is probably that it is the birthplace of the giant Greyhound Corporation, which today operates more than 4,400 buses over a hundred thousand miles of routes in the United States, Alaska, Canada, and Mexico.

In 1914, horse-drawn vehicles provided most of the transportation in Hibbing except for a few livery autos that were rented at five dollars an hour. Carl Wickman, who had recently emigrated from Sweden, owned one of the delivery cars. He had opened an auto agency, but when his one car didn't sell, he had to do something with it, so he put it out to hire.

One day he had an inspiration. People were always traveling back and forth between Hibbing and nearby Alice. Wickman decided to operate his car hourly on a regular schedule between these two towns. The day after he began, he made a sign and started his little one-man, one-vehicle, bus line. Folks soon knew they could catch his car in front of the saloon in Hibbing and fifteen minutes later get off at the firehouse in Alice. The fare was fifteen cents one way, twenty-five cents round trip. Soon passengers not only filled the car but clung to the running boards and fenders.

Seeing Wickman's success, one of his competitors, Ralph Bogan, decided to operate over the same route and at the same rates. Wickman's business fell off when he had to share it with Bogan and a price war followed until Wickman suggested that instead of fighting each other, they join forces. Bogan agreed, and the new partners combined their capital and equipment. Soon they were building more buses and extending their operations south until they reached the city of Minneapolis.

At the time that the partners were pushing their little bus line farther out of Hibbing, Wickman met another young man who had been an auto mechanic, owned an auto agency, and was now operating a bus line running out of Superior, Wisconsin. Wickman persuaded Orville S. Caesar to join forces with Bogan and himself. Thereafter, the three embarked on a steady program of buying up bus lines, integrating them into their existing operation, and at the same time steadily extending their routes in all directions.

Nothing stopped them during these busy years of growth in the early 1920s. They hopped over state lines, pushed across rivers, and conquered the highest mountain ranges, constantly pushing out into new territories. The only barriers Wickman, Bogan, and Caesar acknowledged were the Atlantic and Pacific oceans and the Mexican border (because there were no good roads beyond that point). During this period the trio called their business the Motor Transit Company, although some of its bus lines operated under more colorful names.

It was from one of the little lines, a company in western Michigan that had joined up with Wickman and his associates, that the Greyhound name came. A sketch of a racing greyhound was painted on the side of each bus, and patrons referred to it as "the Greyhound line." The name appealed to Wickman and the others as singularly appropriate, and it was adopted quickly for the entire system. That was in 1926.

As early as 1940 plans were made for a revolutionary new bus, the Scenicruiser, but due to the war, it was not until 1954 that this forty-foot, double-decker bus with washroom facilities, twin diesels, air suspension, and other comforts appeared on the nation's highways.

The same year the Scenicruiser appeared, Wickman died, leaving Caesar as president and Bogan as executive vice-president. For thirty years these men had worked together and nurtured their baby until it attained the maturity and status of a major corporation. No longer was it owned by the original trio but by more than sixty thousand stockholders. With pride the company called itself "the world's largest passenger transportation company."

Arthur S. Genet, vice-president of the Chesapeake and Ohio Railroad, was elected president of Greyhound in 1956. He made a sweeping reorganization of the company and then turned his attention to operations. Profits had dropped at a time when the nation's economy was steadily expanding, and something had to be done to win more passengers.

Step number one toward filling the buses was to go after the people who make business and pleasure trips. Ads aimed at drivers of private cars were designed to win them over to Greyhound for intercity travel.

"It's such a comfort to take the bus—and leave the driving to us," was the text of a singing jingle used extensively. For 1957, Genet's goal was to add one passenger to each schedule.

Greyhound all-expense tours were introduced to attract vacation travelers to events such as the Rose Bowl football game, the Mardi Gras, and other festivals. The first land-sea trip to Hawaii via Greyhound and Matson Navigation Company sold out quickly. Next, Genet met with railroad executives who were anxious to get rid of their unprofitable passenger business, particularly on branch lines. Genet was eager to substitute his buses for short- or long-haul railroad service, except commuting service, which is never profitable.

Genet turned his sights on other kinds of transportation also. It may seem odd, for example, that Genet looked to airline passengers as a good source of business, but consider the situation in Detroit. Airline travelers must take a thirty-five-mile ride on Greyhound to get from the Willow Run Airport to downtown Detroit. Genet found that other airports of major cities were also situated far from the downtown area.

In addition to the above-mentioned expansions, Genet decided it was illogical to think of a bus as capable of carrying only passengers. Why not also haul small packages, newspapers, and the like in the roomy baggage compartments under each bus? As a result of this thinking, Greyhound now offers its Greyhound Package Express, including pickup and delivery service in more than 260 cities in 38 states.

When Gerald Troutman took over the wheel as chairman in 1966, he drove the company down the expansion road taking it to a place among the nation's top one hundred corporations. One of his first moves was to acquire Armour, the giant of the meat packing industry, and then move the company headquarters to Phoenix, Arizona. One company led to another and today computers, equipment leasing, insurance, and banking are but some of the company businesses. In fact, it was once said that if you took a cross-country trip on a Greyhound bus you would pay for your trip with Greyhound money orders, insure your luggage with Greyhound insurance, eat Armour products at Greyhound fast food restaurants, wash with Dial soap, and if you were to look up at the sky, you would possibly see some of the jet aircraft the company owns or leases.

However, this changed in 1986 when Troutman's successor, John W. Teets, disposed of a dozen Greyhound subsidiaries, including Armour and the bus business. Mr. Teets said at the time that selling the mother company was a "gut-wrenching decision." Greyhound took over its largest competitor, Trailways, and survived as a much smaller company devoted solely to providing, for the most part, long-distance bus transportation.

At the 1996 annual stockholders meeting, President Craig R. Lentzsch said in part: "I think our future is going to be bright . . . we do believe that our market is growing." His optimism was based on the company lowering fares and the fact that travelers were taking more and more long-haul trips. The nation's large populations of senior citizens, African-Americans, and Hispanics were expected to grow during the next twenty-five years, and he was confident they would continue to be among Greyhound's primary customers.

Greyhound has come a long way since that first trip Carl Wickman made in his Hupmobile. From carrying a few dozen passengers a day in 1912, the Greyhound Corporation has become the largest intercity carrier of passengers in the nation.

A LOOK AT THE BUS INDUSTRY

Buses provide many communities with their only means of public transportation to and from the outside world. Those who live in large cities may find that the bus is a convenient alternative to air and rail travel. In fact, over short distances, such as between Boston and Providence, or New York and Philadelphia, your bus may prove almost as fast as a plane or train, and the service may be more frequent. Bus terminals are usually located in the heart of the city, whereas the railroad station may not be as convenient. In addition, there are those bus lines that provide intrastate service (operate wholly within one state) and companies that offer charter or other special services to the public.

Unlike other forms of transportation, which need to maintain stations or terminals with a number of workers at each stop where passengers board or leave their planes or trains, buses are uniquely able to eliminate this expense in most of the communities they serve. The corner garage, drugstore, or newsstand serves as a waiting room for passengers, and the owner sells tickets and provides travel information. These arrangements cut down on the number of employees required to operate a rural bus system.

It does not take a mathematical genius to realize that apart from the leader in the industry, Greyhound, the other companies offer limited employment opportunities. Openings would be mostly for clerical positions, some ticket agents, mechanics to service and repair the vehicles, cleaners, and perhaps a few custodians if the bus line operated its own terminal. Openings will vary according to the size of a company and the complexity of its operations. The very largest operators might offer additional employment possibilities for dispatchers, computer specialists, accountants, and applicants with an economics and/or statistical background. These last two specialties might qualify applicants as forecasters, rate and schedule specialists, and financial analysts. So-called professionals, public relations specialists, attorneys, and business librarians would find little or no real opportunities in this area.

Since the business of transporting passengers by bus is uncomplicated, a small company can operate profitably with a half dozen buses, a few drivers, and as many other employees as needed to keep the books, sell tickets, and service the vehicles. For most companies it is a "bus and driver" business. The driver is the most important employee in the business because he or she is the operator of the bus, and to the passenger that person is the company. Almost 60 percent of Greyhound's employees are drivers; therefore, if you would like to enter this industry and you enjoy driving, give careful consideration to the possibility of becoming a driver.

Nature of the Work

You have completed your training and are proudly wearing your new uniform as an important member, a driver, of the company team. What would you do on the first day you report for work?

Upon arriving at the garage or terminal where you are assigned a bus, you pick up tickets, report forms, and other items needed for your trip. Then you find your bus and inspect the vehicle to make certain that the steering mechanism, brakes, windshield wipers, lights, and mirrors are working properly. Then you check the fuel, water, oil, and tires and see that the necessary safety equipment is on board. This includes first aid kits, fire extinguishers, and emergency reflectors.

Your inspection completed, you drive to the loading dock, and if there is no porter to help load the baggage, you stand near the door to collect tickets, check bags, and store them in the luggage compartment. You might use the terminal's public address system to announce the destination, route, time of departure and arrival at the next stop, and other information. At departure time you settle into your seat, turn on the ignition switch, and go.

If yours is a local run, you probably will stop at many small towns only a few miles apart. At each stop you help passengers leave and board the bus, unload and load baggage, and take tickets. If it is an express run, you will probably drive several hours on an interstate or other highway before making your first stop. En route you will regulate the lighting, heating, and air-conditioning equipment. Should you get a flat or something goes wrong with the engine, it is your job to change the tire and, if possible, fix the motor, if repair service is not available.

At your destination, you discharge your passengers, drive the bus to the garage, or turn it over to the next driver, and then prepare your reports. The U.S. Department of Transportation requires drivers to keep a record of each trip. The following is recorded: distance traveled, periods of time off duty, and time spent performing other duties. You also must report any repairs or special servicing the bus might need, and it is possible that your employer expects you to complete certain company reports as well.

If you drive a chartered bus, you pick up a group of people, take them to whatever destination is set on the schedule, and remain with them until they are ready to return. Some charter buses are used for organized tours, in which case you would stay away from home for one or more nights.

Should you drive an intercity bus, you can expect to work at all hours of the day and night, every day of the year. As a new driver you will be on call at all hours and may have to report for work on short notice. If you are away from home overnight there will be a meal allowance and possibly reimbursement of your hotel expense. Driving schedules range from six to ten hours a day and from three and a quarter to six days a week, but under U.S. Department of Transportation regulations you cannot, as an intercity driver, drive more than ten hours without at least eight consecutive hours off. Although driving is not physically difficult, it is tiring and calls for steady nerves. You alone are responsible for the safety of your passengers and bus, and that calls for an alert mind.

Greyhound Requirements

Here is what the Greyhound Corporation has expected of its applicants:

1. Applicants must be between twenty-four and thirty-five years of age.
2. Applicants must have at least 20/40 vision with or without corrective lenses.
3. Applicants must pass the Greyhound preemployment physical examination; applicants must have weight proportionate to height (to be determined by the company doctor).
4. Applicants must have no more than two moving violations and/or accidents in the last three years and no suspension or revocation within the last three years. They must have no more than four moving violations and/or accidents in the last five years or one suspension or revocation within the last five years.
5. Applicants must meet all applicable federal and state requirements.
6. Applicants must have an acceptable employment record and demonstrate mature judgment and good character.

To become a bus driver you must successfully complete Greyhound's driver training school. Prior experience as a bus driver is not required.

Long before it became the popular thing to do, Greyhound was an equal opportunity employer. Through the years, not only has Greyhound insisted on fair and equal treatment of minority groups using its services, but it has tried to ensure the same impartiality regarding employment in the company. Employment inquiries should be directed to your local Greyhound Company operated terminal.

A Few Other Important Facts

It should be noted that in some companies those drivers with low seniority may be laid off temporarily during the winter when traffic drops. Most intercity drivers belong to one of three unions: the Amalgamated Transit Union, the United Transportation Union, or the International Brotherhood of Teamsters.

Salary scales vary tremendously, however. In 1994 median weekly earnings of bus drivers who worked full time were $401. The middle 50 percent earned between $291 and $610 a week. Local transit bus drivers received a top hourly wage of $16.74 from companies with more than 1,000 employees, and wage scales were less for smaller companies. Intercity bus drivers, who were beginners and worked six months out of the year, earned about $22,000, whereas many senior drivers who worked all year earned more than $48,000.

It would seem that local bus service feeding into large cities where passengers can connect with long-distance carriers should be on the increase, since it can be operated with small and relatively inexpensive equipment. This would spread career opportunities throughout many areas and brighten job prospects for those interested in this vital transportation service.

For the addresses of local bus companies, see the yellow pages in your phone directory. You can also find the names and addresses of most bus companies and get an idea of the size of each by looking in the *Motor Coach Guide*. If this is unavailable at a local bus station, travel agency, or public library, contact your state employment service for assistance.

CHAPTER 5

THE RAILROAD REVIVAL

A year after the Erie Canal opened in 1825, the nation's first railroad began hauling blocks of granite cut from a quarry in Quincy, Massachusetts, to the Neponsit River. There the stone was loaded on boats and floated some ten miles over to Charlestown to be used for constructing the Bunker Hill Monument. A second and similar railroad opened the following year in Pennsylvania to transport anthracite coal. However, it was left to the Baltimore and Ohio Railroad to become the nation's oldest from the standpoint of offering continuous passenger service starting in 1830.

During the 1830s numerous other railroads were laying primitive rails in various parts of the Atlantic coast states. At first most of them provided shuttle service between two cities or towns; a few served as connecting links to two canals, which otherwise could not offer their shippers through service. The latter part of the 1830s witnessed an epidemic of railroad construction with many of today's major lines tracing their origins back to that time. Although by 1840 only 1,098 miles of track had been laid, the public understood the importance of these pioneering companies and what they portended. Soon one canal after another went out of business, and further major road construction and repair were greatly reduced. Railroads were seen as the answer to all transportation needs.

The railroad fever raced throughout the country until the 1870s when investors feared there had been too much expansion. The resulting stock market Railroad Panic of 1873 brought such a crash in stock values that further construction practically halted until the 1880s. Then more mileage was added than during any previous decade!

Now the west was host to most of the new trackage. By this time in the east two or more companies were competing for passenger and freight traffic between most principal cities. After 1916 additional expansion fell off dramatically, and thereafter many railroad companies were finding it increasingly difficult to make a profit except during World War II. Not only was there fierce competition but there was also insufficient traffic on numerous branch lines that were no longer profitable.

From here on the story has been mostly one of railroads losing business to airlines, buses, and trucks, abandoning unprofitable main and branch lines, and merging with other companies in a desperate struggle to survive. Finally two premier long-time rival lines, New York Central and Pennsylvania, merged and then failed. Ironically this helped create a new day for railroading because the government stepped in to save the transportation crisis in the east by helping give birth to two new rail systems: Amtrak and Conrail.

AMTRAK'S NEW METROLINER EXPRESS SERVICE

Imagine this if you will:

You're speeding to Washington on the all-new Metroliner Express Service. Your scheduled running time: a remarkable 2 hours and 59 civilized minutes.

Your body is relaxing in a big, wide, comfortable reclining seat. The new, roomier 60-seat car creates an incredible amount of space all around you.

You pull up your leg rest, settle back, do some work, read. Later, you decide to stroll to the lounge car and you select from a menu that is better than ever. Hot meals. Cold snacks. Wine. Beer. Cocktails.

Or imagine that you opted for our new club car service.

Now you're enjoying a complimentary Continental breakfast. Or a light meal for lunch or dinner.

Or perhaps you wish to order from the menu. Here you peruse a variety of entrees, and you are served at your seat.

While you're dining you realize that you are now experiencing all the luxuries the Washington business traveler has long since given up.

But it's all happening now—speed and comfort—on Amtrak. Downtown to downtown. From Penn Station four times a day, every business day. To Washington. And back. (Plus there's also all-new service on our six other Metroliner trains every business day.)

The above advertisement, which appeared in the *New York Times,* is indicative of the new look that Amtrak is assuming. The "prophets of doom" who say that railroading is obsolete should ride one of these fine trains or some of the other Amtrak limiteds, or watch one of the Conrail freights speed by. They will agree that railroads are not only here to stay but could have an exciting future.

Unfortunately, America's total rail mileage has shrunk considerably over the past fifty years as many unprofitable branches and even main lines were abandoned. As railroad companies merged or went out of business, most of the once luxurious passenger services disappeared. Suburban commuter services—which are operated for the most part by independent authorities created by the state or local government—can continue because of state government subsidies.

To understand the railroad picture, let's take a closer look at the two government-sponsored railroad corporations: Amtrak and Conrail.

AMTRAK AND CONRAIL

Amtrak

By 1970 more than 100 of the nation's 500 passenger railroads had asked the Interstate Commerce Commission for permission to discontinue all service. Since 1950 most of these privately owned companies had been operating their trains at a loss and were facing bankruptcy. The automobile, which could now speed over the new interstate highway system as well as other improved roads, provided a less expensive and more flexible form of transportation for many families that had formerly traveled by train. At the same time the growth of airline service and the speed of the jets, which could fly coast-to-coast in less than six hours, contrasted heavily with the three-day train trip, making transcontinental rail service practically obsolete. True, some people still preferred to ride trains or were afraid to fly, but there were not enough of them.

In October 1970 Congress established Amtrak, officially known as the National Railroad Passenger Corporation. This was a quasi-public corporation, its board of directors composed of eight officers appointed by the president, three representatives from the railroad industry, and four private investors. These investors were chosen from those who held the company's preferred stock.

Congress intended the company to be a profit-making enterprise and gave it an initial grant of $40 million plus $100 million in federal loan guarantees. By the time Amtrak began operating in 1971, it had eliminated half of the intercity passenger service, keeping only those trains that enjoyed dense traffic. During that first year, trains were running over 180 routes and serving approximately 300 cities. Amtrak is the only intercity carrier. In addition, there are about twenty regional commuter carriers and numerous excursion rail carriers that operate over short trackage.

For years Japan and France have led the railroad world with their high-speed passenger trains. In March 1996 the United States took steps to join them as Amtrak announced plans to order eighteen new trainsets that would allow it to cut 25–30 percent off scheduled times between Boston and Washington. First, however, the Boston-New Haven section must be electrified and tracks, bridges, and signals upgraded for the new speedy service. Since Amtrak serves downtown centers in each major city, it will be able to compete with airlines that must use airports usually located some distance out of town.

High-speed rail service for the entire New England corridor—Boston to Washington—at speeds up to 150 miles per hour will give rail travel a new profile. High-speed trains between Miami and Orlando, Florida, and Los Angeles and San Diego are also in the planning stage, but the realization of these dreams will depend on whether the necessary funding can be obtained.

Conrail

Following the bankruptcy of the Penn-Central Railroad, the largest business failure in American history, Congress created the Consolidated Rail Corp., otherwise known as Conrail. The legislation became effective on April 1, 1976. From the ruins of six bankrupt railroads, it put together a 17,000-mile system that served seventeen states and two Canadian provinces. It became the second-largest freight line in the country. By the end of that year, the new company had spent a billion dollars repairing about 12,000 freight cars and 500 locomotives and rehabilitating worn out and dangerous tracks. Nine years later, there were only 14,000 miles of track in fifteen states, assets worth $6 billion, and a payroll of 39,000 employees.

For several years after 1976 Conrail operated at a loss; it was estimated that the railroad was costing taxpayers $1.8 million a day in subsidies. This was a staggering cost, but the railroad is vital to the nation's economy. Then, in 1981, the railroad made a profit that grew in the subsequent years. Nevertheless, the government was eager to dispose of the railroad to private interests, so on March 25, 1987, Conrail sold 58,750,000 shares of stock to the public, netting the government $1.88 billion. Conrail, now a privately owned—not government owned—rail system, is essentially the same railroad that the trustees of the old Penn-Central Railroad tried to create before it went bankrupt.

Commuter Railroads

While it is true that the early trolleys made it possible for city dwellers to move out to less congested areas, later the railroads greatly extended the distance people could conveniently travel to their homes from metropolitan centers. Today most large cities offer good commuting rail service, usually operated by metropolitan or regional authorities. In some cases the railroads contract to run the trains, in others the authority may lease or even purchase the tracks and stations and is responsible for train operation. Because these services are so essential year-round, they offer secure jobs usually with good incomes. Contact the personnel office of the railroad or authority in your city for employment information.

THE MAJOR RAIL LINES

Although the future seemed clouded for Amtrak and Conrail, many of the larger stockholder-owned railroads were prospering in varying degrees. With past and contemplated mergers of large lines, the prospect of fewer but more efficient railroads was encouraging to many shippers, which are the lifeblood of railroads now that passenger service is operated mostly by Amtrak.

In 1980 Staggers Rail Act reduced much of the former government red tape and interference with railroad operation, making trains much more competitive with trucks and water carriers. It allowed railroads to sign long-term contracts in return for guaranteed volume, which meant lower rates for the shippers and steady business for the carriers. Railroads could at last change their rates when necessary to meet the competition without waiting months or years for government approval. This change enabled them to attract business from the highways for the first time.

One area where this was especially beneficial was in the so-called *piggyback* business. This term refers to the movement of truck trailers and containers on rail flatcars. Instead of waiting for Interstate Commerce Commission permission to increase or lower rates for this kind of business, Conrail and the other roads can now match truck rates and initiate their own price changes daily, if necessary.

Just as some of the large truckers keep close track of their trucks, the railroads are improving their ability to spot freight cars wherever they may be. This is important to shippers who often must know where their goods are and when they will be delivered. More important, of course, is a railroad's ability to deliver the freight on schedule, when promised, and at cost competitive with other forms of ground transportation.

By the start of the 1980s it appeared that the railroads' share of total freight ton miles was growing, and with it was growing the companies' operating incomes. Increasing shipments of coal from mines in both the West and the East helped business. As some of the western carriers negotiated the purchase of oil- and coal-producing properties, economists forecast an even more profitable future for railroads.

One of the smaller but more interesting railroads worth noting is the Alaska Railroad, which is owned by the State of Alaska.

The Alaska Railroad

If you land at Seward, which is on Resurrection Bay, and plan to travel up to Fairbanks, undoubtedly you will want to go by rail. At the station your train, made up of four modern coaches pulled by a diesel, is waiting for you. At the conductor's signal the train starts off smoothly, proceeding inland to stop at Portage, then winds around Cook Inlet, and halts briefly at Anchorage to take on more passengers. From here the engine with its cars starts its long climb, passing eleven stations and crossing over the shoulder of Mount McKinley. Then it descends to the flats, where the track leads into Fairbanks. It is a 470-mile, 12-hour winding trip through wilderness, and if you look at a map of Alaska you will note that the Alaska Railroad serves only a very small part of the state. Nevertheless, the railroad's statistics are impressive:

Within the past few years, some 60,000 passengers rode annually between Anchorage and Fairbanks and 100,000 on the twelve-mile branch line between Portage and Whittier. Trains disappear into a tunnel on this line when they pass beneath the Portage glacier. The railroad provides the only direct transportation between these two cities.

On January 2, 1985, the federal government sold the road to the state of Alaska for $22.3 million, together with 38,000 acres of land; buildings worth $13 million; 1,870 cars (mostly freight); and 57 locomotives. Thus Alaska became the first state to own a railroad, which it hoped to extend to lands north of Anchorage over "some rough country" to increase its revenues.

Recognizing the need for safe and reliable tourist and regular passenger service to remote areas, especially during the cold and stormy winter months, the Federal Railroad Administration granted the Alaskan Railroad a $10 million grant in 1996 to upgrade the tracks. A recent innovation was the summertime auto/passenger shuttle from Portage to Whittier port, an unusual service similar to Amtrak's profitable Lorton, Virginia, to Sanford, Florida, successful year-round auto train.

During a recent year the railroad employed about 525 permanent employees and over 100 temporary workers for expanded maintenance of way programs during the few mild summer months. Of these, some forty were young Alaskan high school students acting as on-board tour guides and providing hospitality to passengers. Although employment prospects are not encouraging, if railroading in such an environment interests you, write the Manager, Personnel, The Alaska Railroad, Pouch 7-2111, Anchorage, AK 99510.

SHORT-LINE RAILROADS

Short-line railroads, which are run for tourists and/or railroad buffs, operate in various parts of the country. Probably the two best known are the Mount Washington and the Pikes Peak cog railways. These are seasonal operations that employ about two dozen men and women each. Many of them are college students interested in learning about railroading and earning money for their education. In addition, there are numerous restored rail lines over which steam or diesel power pulls a wide variety of equipment ranging from antique passenger cars to refurbished commuter coaches.

Most of the miniature roads are staffed by railroad buffs who work for the fun of it, but jobs on such lines provide experience as well as an opportunity to learn whether railroading is for you. If interested, write to your state public utility commission for a list of such railroads and inquire about employment opportunities as early as possible.

What is undoubtedly the nation's most unusual railroad operates through the world's third-longest railroad tunnel. The Henderson mine produces molybdenum ore some 5,000 feet and more below the peak of Red Mountain just east of the Continental Divide in Colorado. A short-line railroad takes the ore from the mine.

The double-track road starts deep within the mine at 7,500 feet above sea level where the ore cars are loaded. The electric powered trains proceed through the 9.6-mile tunnel to the portal where the tracks extend another 4.8 miles on the surface to the processing plant. Electric locomotives are at each end of a train, and with two more in the middle, they can power thirty ore cars. A round-trip requires a little over an hour and a half.

About 1,900 men and women are employed at the mine, which operates on a seven-day, around-the-clock schedule. Although there are numerous job opportunities in a variety of areas, those involved in transportation are quite limited. If you are interested, write: AMAX Inc., Public Relations, Henderson Mine, Empire, CO 80438.

EMPLOYMENT

Railroads employ about 82 percent of all railroad workers according to the *Occupational Outlook Handbook.* The balance work for local transit companies and manufacturing and mining companies that operate their own railroad equipment. According to 1994 estimated figures, employment consisted of the following: brake operators, 19,000; conductors, 26,000; locomotive engineers, 22,000; and yard engineers and dinkey operators, 6,000.

Employment of transit (bus, street car, and subway) workers is expected to grow faster than the average as cities expand or build new transit systems. On the other hand all occupations in railroad transportation are expected to decline through the year 2005.

The once-familiar sight of a veteran engineer leaning out the cab window, hand on the throttle and eyes straining ahead to see the next signal, inspired many a child to become a locomotive engineer. Then airplane pilots replaced steam locomotive engineers as heroes for young boys. The advent of the diesel locomotive further eroded the romantic appeal of railroading. Nevertheless, the haunting train whistle echoing through the valley to the pounding of the heavy driving wheels is not altogether gone.

Equal employment opportunity means that now you can look up at the cab of a speeding diesel and possibly see a woman at the throttle. Today, railroading is open to everyone, and though the nostalgia of the old steam engine is gone, some young people are attracted to the prospect of running diesel and electric engines.

Many look with equal enthusiasm at the career possibilities that exist elsewhere in railroad companies. Let's see what employment opportunities there may be for you in the three principal divisions of a railroad. Space limitations make it necessary to sketch the positions briefly.

Administrative

Railroads are no different from other industries that require a wide variety of clerical and other office personnel. Accordingly you will find tire usual secretaries and clerks performing specialized duties. Then there are employees working in the advertising, computer, labor relations, legal, personnel, public relations, purchasing, and sales departments. Other specialists are scattered throughout the entire organization.

Maintenance

Making certain that engines, freight and passenger cars, as well as tracks, signals, and communications equipment are in perfect working order is the responsibility of this division. Because trains operate around the clock, continuous attention must be paid to every part of the operation.

Included among the specialized jobs in this division is that of car repairer. That person may be assigned to check rolling stock as it comes into a terminal or work in the repair shop performing necessary maintenance or major overhauls. Mechanics are assigned to diesel engines and other motorized equipment while electricians repair and service electrical equipment in locomotives and cars. They also work on air conditioners and other electrical apparatuses. A variety of skilled workers make repairs on motors, and engine and car frames; replace parts such as fuel lines, air hoses, valves, and wheels; or rebuild engine transmissions.

Out on the right-of-way, gangs of workers replace rails and ties and tamp down ballast to keep tracks in top condition. Others repair and paint bridges, clean culverts, and dig ditches alongside the roadbed. Much of this work is now performed by intricate machinery, which decreases the need for the large section gangs. Some employees are required to operate the machines, however.

Communications are important to safe operations. Trained maintenance workers service the all-important signal system. They also repair the telephone, radio, and microwave systems. Radio is used so that engineers can talk with their conductors a mile away in the caboose, and personnel can communicate with each other in the yards and between stations.

Transportation

These are the men and women who run the trains: engineers, brake operators (formerly called brakemen), and conductors. In the days of the coal-fired steam engines, a fireman was an important member of the engine crew. With the advent of diesels, the services of a fireman were eliminated.

Engineers operate locomotives in passenger, freight, or yard service. Passenger trains run on tight schedules, and it is the engineer's job to reach each station on time. If the train is delayed by red signals or for other reasons, he or she tries to make up for lost time without sacrificing safety.

Freight engineers pilot freight trains, which may be either fast freights operating on set schedules or local freights that pick up and drop cars at way stations. They, too, operate according to a schedule but are not necessarily held to it because the number of cars to be switched varies from day to day.

Yard engineers who run the switching engines make up trains by sorting out cars and pulling or pushing them to the tracks where they will be coupled together to form new trains.

Brake operators ride on the trains, one in the caboose with the conductor, the other up in front in the cab with the engineer. In the old days before the air brake was invented, brakemen were what their name implies. They operated the hand brakes on freight and passenger cars on a signal from the engineer. It was dangerous work, running back and forth on top of swaying freight cars in icy or snowy weather. It is still dangerous because when a freight train approaches a siding to pick up or drop cars, the brake operator jumps off the engine and runs ahead to set the switches.

The brake operator also couples and uncouples cars at terminals, stations, and sidings. In the yards the brake operator couples and uncouples cars, and throws switches. He or she often climbs up a car to ride with it and control its speed with the hand brake as it rolls down an incline to be joined with a series of cars that are being made up into a train.

Brake operators on passenger trains have it much easier. They watch over the operation of the cars and their equipment. They also use flags and flares to protect the train from a rear end collision whenever the train is forced to make an unscheduled stop.

Conductors are in charge of trains, whether passenger, freight, or yard. The yard conductors supervise the workers and make up trains.

Working Conditions

Most train crew members do not have a regular five-day week. Railroad assignments are made on the basis of seniority. The more years you have worked, the more you have to say about when you want to work. New employees may be on call twenty-four hours a day, never knowing when they will be called to report for duty.

Those employed in the office, the shops, and out on the tracks usually have regular shifts. During the snow months section gangs may work overtime clearing the switches and tracks. In the event of an accident or other emergency, they may be called out to work nights and weekends.

Education and Training

A high school diploma is the minimum educational requirement for the majority of railroad jobs. One of the best things about railroading is that in most assignments you learn on the job and may be taught by a skilled worker.

For the jobs in the maintenance and transportation division, some railroads seek trained applicants. Others train you on the job, depending on the position.

Conductors are chosen from the ranks of brake operators. Engineers may serve first as engineers' helpers to obtain training, and then take substitute assignments as engineers. Engineers must have sufficient knowledge of train service rules to pass an examination on the operation of diesel or electric locomotives.

To qualify for their jobs, conductors, brake operators, and engineers must be able to pass examinations showing that they have satisfactory hearing, eyesight, and color vision, and the ability to exercise good judgment. Once employed in these positions they must be able to pass periodic physical exams.

Perhaps a sign of a brighter future for railroads and all transportation was an advertisement of CSX Corporation, "the company that puts things in motion," which employed 60,000, including the Chessie System and the Seaboard System. The full-page advertisement showed a tugboat pulling several barges beneath which was a large headline reading: "Watching One of Our Trains Go By." In smaller type, at the bottom of the advertisement, the following copy appeared:

If you think we're just a railroad, take another look.

We're a lot more. We're American Commercial Barge Lines, the country's largest inland waterway transportation company.

That's not all. We're also container ships. Trucks. Pipelines. Energy resources. Fiber optics. Resorts and property development. And, of course, the railroad. And we're developing new technology to make it all work together.

We're CSX, the first true global transporter. If you've never heard of one before, it's because there's never been one before. This is a company on the move.

After many discouraging years, Amtrak, Conrail, and the stockholder-owned freight carriers are experiencing a new burst of business and optimism. Once threatened by the trucking industry and its use of the interstate highway system, railroads have displayed imagination and instituted innovative programs to recapture or keep their share of the nation's passenger and freight business. No better example of this is Amtrak's courageous plunge into the high-speed rail service, which should put it on par with bus and airline competition. The future for the nation's rail industry looks bright.

For further information write the Office of Information and Public Affairs, Association of American Railroads, 50 F Street, NW, Washington, DC 20001-1564.

CHAPTER 6

THE UNDERGROUND PIPELINE EMPIRE

The Chinese built the first known pipeline about one thousand years ago, using bamboo pipes to carry natural gas to use for various purposes including evaporating salt brine. One of the next recorded uses of pipes was a Roman gravity water supply system of almost four hundred miles that brought water over aqueducts and through pipes to Rome. Pumps were used in 1582 to propel London's water supply through that large city. Most early pipes were of wooden construction, and doubtless there was considerable leakage at joints due to rot and ground settling. Today cities throughout the world use metal and concrete pipes to bring water from distant points and distribute it to a wide variety of users.

As growing cities must reach out farther and farther to tap new water sources, pipelines become longer and longer. The huge pipeline that brings Colorado River water all the way to Los Angeles is a good example.*

Pipelines provide the cheapest and most efficient method of overland transportation. Because they are laid mostly underground, there is little wear and tear on the pipes. They are protected not only from the elements but also from vandalism. The power sources, pumps, and compressors are stationary, and best of all, piping is free of the unprofitable

---

*Although transporting gas and petroleum is our chief interest here, note should be made of job opportunities in those cities and towns that must obtain water from outside sources and distribute it. Inquire at your local water department about possible employment opportunities.

"return trip" required of railroad cars, trucks, and ships. Pipelines do not require handling, containers, terminals, or the need to keep extra vehicles or boats on hand to cover a breakdown or other emergency.

NATURAL GAS PIPELINES

The early discovery and history of natural gas is as mysterious as the three-thousand-year-old account of the Greek oracle at Delphi, where the steady burning fire caused by natural gas escaping from a rock lent credibility to the messages received from the gods. Subsequently in many parts of the world, gas was similarly set afire as it seeped from cracks in rock, and the flames' significance was interpreted one way or another according to local beliefs.

In Colonial America many knew of such fires, and rumor even had it that at one time George Washington owned land that had "a burning spring." Since wood and waterpower were the principal energy sources, no one saw any utility in this phenomenon until 1820, when William Hart drilled down twenty-seven feet next to a rock crack venting gas. He hoped to increase the amount of vapor by widening the hole. His idea was so successful that he managed to pipe the gas to adjacent homes and stores. Thus Fredonia, New York, a small town near Buffalo, became the first village lit by gas, and its fame became so great that on his second American tour, the Marquis de Lafayette visited the hamlet to see this wonder.

In 1870 gas first flowed from Fredonia through a twelve and one-half inch wooden pipeline to Rochester. Actually the inside diameter was only eight and one-half inches, which encouraged pipeline designers to devise a two-inch-diameter iron pipe that was laid from a wellhead in Titusville, Pennsylvania, to transport gas to buyers some 5.5 miles out of town.

During the following two decades, small companies started to ship gas to numerous industries in New York, Ohio, Pennsylvania, and West Virginia using eight-inch wrought-iron pipe capable of withstanding eighty pounds per-square-inch pressure. Soon a long-distance delivery system began operating in 1891 as two parallel lines sent gas 120 miles from northern Indiana to Chicago. Elsewhere in Arkansas, Kansas, Louisiana, Missouri, and Texas, numerous short distribution companies appeared, and by 1920 new markets were opened thanks to the seamless, electrically welded pipes of greater length and strength. Thus gas could be sent faster and in larger quantities over greater distances than ever before. Today one of the longest is the pipeline that extends 4,000 miles from western Siberia to several European countries.

The owner of a gas pipeline is a marketing concern, buying gas from producers at the wellheads and selling it to the industry and local utilities, which in turn distribute it to schools, hospitals, businesses, and residential users. During the 1970s gas pipeline operators worried about providing adequate quantities for their customers and being able to meet demands for gas, especially after the Arab countries shut off the oil supply.

The 1980s brought different problems. The pipeline companies had adequate supplies of gas to draw on, but there was fierce competition with oil and coal suppliers. Furthermore, in 1986 Congress deregulated federal rules that had formerly guaranteed companies a certain rate of return. Finally, some of the gas companies had numerous long-term contracts requiring them to sell gas at a loss because costs of transporting it had risen since the agreements were signed. This was not true of the entire industry, however, and some companies were making a profit.

The 1986 deregulation started a revolution in the natural-gas pipeline industry. At first large steel plants, which were major gas customers, were able to make their own price agreements with suppliers. In 1993 pipeline companies had to make their lines available to competing gas suppliers through leasing arrangements. Thus, instead of having to buy their gas from the local utility company that had installed the pipes leading to homes and businesses, customers could purchase it from other gas marketers, who might offer lower rates, and use the existing gas lines that were originally laid by the local utility.

Groups of residential customers will be able to choose any gas marketer they want, which will force the utility now serving them to reduce its rates to meet the new competition. The industry is joining the electric power and telephone companies, which have also been forced to lease their electric lines and phone cables to competitors. Instead of enjoying a monopoly as they have since they started in business, local utilities will face competition, and this will result in significant savings for the public as well as business and industry.

Long-term prospects for the gas industry are good. "The clean fuel" creates no environmental problems like coal and oil. Since the United States has ample reserves there is no danger of a foreign supplier turning off the valves, as was the case with oil in 1973 when the Arab countries' embargo cut petroleum imports drastically and created a serious energy problem for many Americans.

A LOOK AT THE GAS PIPELINES

Gas is obtained from special wells driven into the ground. The vapor goes from the ground to a separation unit where various gases, liquids, and impurities are removed. Then the gas goes directly by pipeline to users or underground storage areas.

For a better idea of what it takes to lay a gas pipeline, let's turn back the calendar to 1943 when the government urgently needed additional energy in West Virginia for the war effort.

Tennessee Gas and Transmission Company

As America's industrial arsenal grew during World War II, defense plants in the Appalachian area began to run out of fuel and were in danger of falling behind their production schedules. Natural gas reserves were limited, and coal production could not keep pace with industry's needs. However, some 1,200 miles away, the Chicago Corporation, which owned a large natural gas reserve, was seeking a market for its underground surplus.

At the request of the War Production Board, the Federal Power Commission issued a certificate permitting construction of a natural gas pipeline from South Texas to West Virginia. The authorization was issued in September 1943 to a new subsidiary of the Chicago Corporation called Tennessee Gas and Transmission Company. In making the authorization, the War Production Board had stipulated that the 1,265-

mile-long pipeline must be completed for operation during the winter of 1944–45.

The fledgling Tennessee Gas and Transmission Company had to assemble an organization, find the necessary materials, hire surveyors and workers to prepare 1,265 miles of right-of-way, let contracts, and construct the twenty-four-inch pipeline, all in record time in order to meet the deadline. In addition, they had to do all this at a time when materials and labor were practically unobtainable.

The first payroll was set up on October 1, 1943, with only a few names on it. Only five weeks after these first employees started work, all but one of the construction contracts had been let. On December 4, ground was broken at the Cumberland River in Tennessee, and the first mainline pipe was welded less than a month later.

The work had scarcely begun, however, before bad weather set in. By May 1 only 76 miles or roughly six percent of the 1,265-mile pipeline had been built. The heavy rain in construction areas turned normally workable terrain into impassible and impossible quagmires. Rocky and mountainous terrain and material shortages added to the mounting problems.

Summer brought improved weather and an increase in the construction pace. In spite of the difficulties and the slow start, the company met its deadline. Gas began moving through the new pipeline on October 31, 1944, less than eleven months from the start of construction. Tennessee Gas had laid more than 1,200 miles of pipeline during wartime, most of it in the last six months at a rate of nearly 7 miles a day. It had secured right-of-way permits from thousands of landowners; crossed sixty-seven rivers and hundreds of roads, highways, and railroads; and built seven pipeline compressor stations. Natural gas, which would have gone unused or been wasted in Texas and Louisiana for lack of a market, was being burned in Appalachian factories where it was badly needed. Tennessee Gas had become an operating company.

In 1966 the company's name was changed to Tenneco, Inc. Today the subsidiary, which bears the company's former corporate name, Tennessee Gas Transmission Company, provides overall administrative and staff services for Tenneco's pipeline network of more than 16,000 miles, over 1.5 million compressor horsepower, in systems operated by four companies.

That original single line has grown into one of the nation's largest interstate pipeline systems, serving utility companies in twenty-five states. More than 85 percent of the gas consumers in Tenneco's populous service area are high priority users—residences, hospitals, schools, and small commercial enterprises. In order to keep these users well-supplied, the company has traditionally relied on the natural gas producing areas of the Gulf Coast. However, existing reserves of gas are declining, and the company is therefore working to develop new reserves. This decline in the nation's domestic reserves of conventional gas is a harsh reality, but the company and others in the gas industry are devoting every effort to develop additional supplies.

One major source of natural gas is the Prudhoe Bay area in northern Alaska. A pipeline was authorized to run south from Prudhoe Bay parallel to the Alaskan oil pipeline to Fairbanks, then east to the Canadian border to join a Canadian-built pipeline extending to the American border. Here one branch would head toward San Francisco and the other to Chicago in order to serve the upper Midwest.

In 1997 it appeared that the pipeline might never be built. The principal reasons were the high construction costs; the cost of the delivered gas, which could not compete with gas sold by other pipeline companies; the difficulty in finding investors for the project; and disagreements over obtaining right-of-way permits through Alaska. Perhaps at some future time, when other supplies of oil, coal, and gas become depleted, this pipeline will become as necessary to the nation as the one Tennessee Gas and Transmission Company laid during World War II.

PETROLEUM PIPELINES

Although pipelines are rarely if ever seen by the public, they are an important part of our transportation system, carrying 24 percent of all intercity freight. Looking at it another way, the 200,000 miles of pipeline total a bit more than all the miles of main line railroad right-of-way.

This vast system consists of two types of pipes: those that deliver crude oil to the refineries; and the smaller "products" pipelines that carry items such as kerosene or gasoline from the refineries. They deliver about 35 percent of all refined petroleum products sold in the United States.

Even before Edwin L. Drake made his famous discovery of oil on his Titusville farm in 1859, barrels of brine oil were being transported from wells in Tarentum, Pennsylvania, to distant points by wagon, boats, and railroad. The cooperage industry enjoyed a sudden boom with the demand for barrels, but it was six years after the black liquid was discovered that the pipeline industry was born.

In western Pennsylvania Sam Van Syckel laid 6 miles of 2-inch pipe from the Pithold Field to the nearest railroad station at Miller's Farm. Now oil could be transported to the railroad at a savings of fifty cents a barrel. Soon other railroads wanted their share of the new business, and additional pipelines were built to carry oil to their tracks. The price competition brought rates down below the Van Syckel costs, and two years later this original company went bankrupt.

This did not deter further development of pipelines, however. In 1869 Tidewater laid the first long-distance line from Coryville in the oil-producing region, all the way to Williamsport. Now some six thousand barrels of crude were flowing each day through the 108-mile, 6-inch pipe up over the Allegheny Mountains. The competition between this and other early lines became so intense that rates for carrying oil dropped to the point where the railroads gave up soliciting long-haul crude oil transportation. Since that time pipelines have been laid throughout the world; most of the world's oil now travels by pipeline from wells to distant tank farms.

When oil was discovered in the Oklahoma and Texas fields during the early 1900s, no one even considered transporting the crude oil by railroad. Companies laid pipelines directly from the wells to refineries and tanker loading ports on the Gulf Coast. Soon sections of pipe were reaching Chicago and the upper Midwest. During the early 1920s the first crude was flowing to the Midwest from the Rocky Mountain area. These lines were usually 8 inches or smaller because larger pipe could not withstand high pressures. If greater capacity was needed, dual pipes would be laid side by side, but the 1930s changed all that.

High-strength and seamless pipe permitted companies to use lines of greater diameter than 8 to 12 inches. Although the larger pipe was more economical to operate, it proved more costly to build. Furthermore, it required more volume to fill than most refiners could provide; hence, two or more companies would join together to build these larger lines, enabling them to meet their total demand.

Oil is moved through pipelines by pumps that push it along at a speed of from 3 to 5 miles an hour. Before World War II pumping stations were spaced at 50-mile intervals along a pipeline, but today 80- or 90-mile spacing is common, and stations may even be as far as 150 miles apart. The distance between pumping stations depends on the diameter of the pipe, the type of oil being moved, and the terrain.

The rate of flow and pumping pressure are controlled completely, regardless of the type of crude or the product or how mountainous the terrain. Warning alarm systems protect the lines as do manual and automatic safety valves, which can close down the line if the pressure drops or rises too drastically. Remotely controlled stations have been installed in recent years, making it possible for an operator to control pumps, valves, regulators, and compressors from one central location.

As many as thirty different shipments may follow one another in close succession through the pipeline. Each shipment or batch is a different petroleum product or grade of crude oil.

Pipelines are patrolled constantly for leaks, which occur infrequently. In the past inspectors walked along the entire pipeline, but today many pipelines are patrolled from the air.

Gas and oil pipelines are similar in their structure. Actually an oil pipeline company is a transportation company. It does not own the product it carries, but merely delivers the petroleum from oil well to refinery. Competition between pipeline corporations for business from potential shippers is so intense that the four largest pipeline companies carry only 46 percent of the total traffic and the eight largest haul but 56 percent. If you think of how few automobile manufacturers, broadcasters, or steel producers there are, you will realize what a competitive industry this is.

Pipeline Transportation Jobs

There are more than three thousand separate occupations in the petroleum industry, but we are concerned here with only those that pertain to pipeline transportation. Amoco Pipeline Company operates 15,700 miles of pipeline, extending from Utah in the west to Indiana in the east, and north to south from the Canadian border to the Gulf of Mexico. The company is a subsidiary of Standard Oil Company (Indiana) and is responsible for transporting petroleum and petroleum products from oil fields and refineries to markets. Discoveries of new fields, declines of older ones, and changes in marketing requirements mean constant changes for the system, as new pipeline is added and existing lines are modernized and revised. Here are the specialist occupations Amoco lists, together with the training required for each:*

Aircraft Patrol Pilot (A)
Aircraft Mechanic (B)
Carpenter Foreman (A)
Chemist (B, X)
Chief Deliveryman (A)
Chief Operator (Pump Station) (A)
Civil Engineer (A, X)
Connection Foreman (A)
Corrosion Engineer (A, X)
Electrician (A)
Foreman (A)
Gager (C, D)

---

*Code: A. Work requiring a high degree of precision, long experience, knowledge of intricate machine operations, special education or unusual aptitude. *B.* Work requiring one year or longer in training, and involving any or all of the following: precision, accuracy, familiarity with specified basic processes, or special education. *C.* Work requiring between six months and one year of training before a new worker is qualified with respect to skill, reliability, or production. *D.* Work requiring less than six months of training before a new or upgraded employee is competent. *X.* Jobs that require four years of college training in a recognized professional school.

Lineman (B)
Loader (D)
Material and Warehouse Supervisor (B)
Mechanic (A)
Mechanical Engineer (A, X)
Operator (B)
Operator (Metering Station) (A)
Pipeline Construction Inspector (A)
Pipeline Crew Foreman (A)
Radio Technician (B)
Right-of-Way and Claims Agent (A)
Shop Foreman (A)
Station Superintendent (A)
Supervisor (Radio Communication) (A)
Tank Foreman (A)
Terminal Man (C)
Tester (Laboratory) (C)
Welder (B)
Welder Foreman (A)
Work Equipment Operator (C)

If you are considering an engineering career, pipeline companies need engineers of various disciplines to handle pipeline construction and operations, according to a company spokesperson. They are interested primarily in holders of bachelor's of science degrees in mechanical, electrical, and civil engineering. Typical assignments include evaluations for new facilities such as crude oil gathering systems, cross-country pipelines, pumping stations, metering installations, and tankage. Their engineers are responsible for electrical and mechanical design, development of material and construction specifications, supervision and inspection of construction, and supervision of operations.

Two typical pipeline positions are those of dispatcher and inspector. Here are brief descriptions of each:

Dispatchers watch over and regulate the flow of natural gas in the pipelines. Sitting before an instrument panel, they can tell how much oil or gas is passing through the pipe as well as its temperature, pressure, and speed. In the case of gas, they may have to decide how much will be needed by customers during the next few hours so there will be an ample supply on hand. They do this after taking into consideration the outside temperature and expected weather conditions, the time of day, and past needs. Then they change the flow by adjusting switches that open or close valves and regulate the speed of compressors, all of which may be located many miles away. In the event of an emergency they must make quick decisions and take appropriate action. Some dispatchers stationed at the end of oil pipelines are responsible for routing the crude through smaller lines to the storage tanks of their numerous customers. Promotion may be to the job of chief dispatcher. This person supervises dispatchers, does long-range planning for the movements of gas or oil through the pipelines, and keeps various records of the operation for departmental accounts, government reports, and other uses.

Inspectors use test equipment as they travel along the pipelines looking for leaks or signs of other problems. Depending on the terrain, they either drive a truck, which contains their equipment, or walk along the buried or above-ground pipe searching for signs of leaks. Some companies use airplanes to patrol those above-ground lines that run through remote areas. In cities, inspectors' work is more complicated as they watch over pipes that run under streets and sidewalks and branch into buildings.

It goes without saying that although the list of Amoco specialist positions did not include the usual office positions open to clerical, financial, sales, public relations, purchasing, and legal personnel, they are as essential to any pipeline company as the engineers, dispatchers, or inspectors.

Employment Outlook

In 1994, approximately 31,000 workers were employed on gas and petroleum plant and systems occupations. Prospects for employment in this industry are not promising, although the natural gas industry is one of the largest employers in the country. Since both the gas and oil industries are essential to the nation's welfare, they are not affected by recessions as much as most other industries. Pay scales are generally high, employee benefits generous, and working conditions on the whole are good. Pipelines are the most important means of delivering gas and oil from wells to customers or refineries. Remember, though, that there are additional employment possibilities with oil companies, since petroleum products are also transported by ship, railroad tank cars, and tank trucks. Although petroleum is not found in every state, practically every city and town has a distributor of oil or petroleum products, and distribution means transportation.

High school graduates have better chances of finding beginning jobs than those without a diploma. If you have had some related part-time experience during summer vacations, it should prove helpful in finding a job. Many companies have their own training programs for new employees, but if you have obtained some technical training, you will find it advantageous when you interview for a job.

Consult the following periodicals for possible advertisements of job openings: *LP-Gas News* and the *Oil and Gas Journal.* If your library does not have subscriptions to them, perhaps you could ask to see issues at the office of your nearest gas or oil distributor. Be sure to contact local employment agencies and your state employment security office.

For further information write the American Petroleum Institute, 1220 L Street, NW, Washington, DC 20005; American Gas Association, 1515 Wilson Boulevard, Arlington, VA 22209; or the Association of Oil Pipe Lines, 1725 K Street, NW, Washington, DC 20006.

CHAPTER 7

OUR LOVE AFFAIR WITH AUTOMOBILES

While it is true that the airplane changed much of the world by making it possible to travel and ship goods between cities and nations in a matter of hours instead of days, weeks, or months, it was the mass production of automobiles that within a few decades brought about the greatest changes in our lifestyles, economy, and environment.

We can be certain that back in 1600 when a Dutchman, Simon Steven, built his "sailing chariot"—a wagon propelled by wind—he was only trying to devise a vehicle that would operate without horsepower, not revolutionize how the world would eventually travel and speed. Obviously when the wind died down the vehicle was useless, which is why in 1796 Nicolas Cugnot used steam to make the first self-propelled vehicle. Frightened by similar developments in England, Parliament passed various laws restricting these steam-powered vehicles. Finally it adopted the Red Flag Act of 1865, which required a rider on horseback to carry a red flag ahead of each such vehicle.

At the beginning of the nineteenth century Oliver Evans, an American, achieved the same success also using steam, but it was not until 1883 that the Duryea brothers used their gas-fired engine to run a carriage through the muddy streets of Springfield, Massachusetts. Two years later a Rochester, New York, lawyer, George B. Selden, patented his internal combustion engine, which was copied by numerous would-be auto inventors, including Henry Ford of Detroit. In 1908 Ford brought out his Model T and in 1913 started mass producing his black "Tin Lizzies." By 1927, when Ford discontinued the Model T for a more modern Model A, the company had produced 15,000,000 cars. As the Model A's came off the assembly lines, most of the independent manufacturers gradually disappeared, and by 1949 Chrysler, Ford, and General Motors were producing 85 percent of all American-made cars.

We have previously seen that the United States had to build a vast network of roads and highways to accommodate the ever-growing number of cars and trucks. A more serious problem gradually developed as the number of gasoline-driven vehicles increased. Gasoline fumes were helping create alarming environmental problems. In many cities where temperature inversion trapped smog for several days, half of the pollutants were attributed to gasoline fumes. At the same time it was suspected that these fumes were also contributing to the greenhouse effect, or heat build-up in the earth's atmosphere. Accordingly California, Maine, Massachusetts, and New York passed laws requiring that starting in 1998 a minimum of 2 percent of all cars sold by a manufacturer in those states be powered by electricity.

Only time will tell how successful these laws will be. Until a battery is developed that can power such a car for more than 100–250 miles on a charge, such models will be useful for the most part only for consumers' daily short trips but not for long-distance runs. Furthermore, few people may be able to afford these expensive cars, although in time, as more are manufactured and sold, the cost should come down. Understandably the oil industry is not enthusiastic over the prospect of electric cars.

IMPORTANCE OF THE AUTOMOBILE INDUSTRY

This book discusses transportation, not manufacturing of the various types of machines or vehicles that carry passengers and cargo. Thus we have not covered shipbuilding or the manufacture of buses, light rail cars, trolleys, airplanes, or railroad equipment. In the case of automobiles and light trucks, however, we are making an exception because career opportunities are vast in the manufacturing plants and are closely tied to various peripheral service businesses that support the industry once automobiles and trucks leave the factories. It is interesting to note that light trucks are starting to dominate the light-vehicle assembly lines. Pickup trucks, minivans, and sports-utility vehicles accounted for 60 percent of Chrysler's total sales early in 1996!

Excluding those who work in agriculture, one out of every seven jobs in the United States is related to the manufacture and use of automobiles and light trucks and gives employment to some 12,000,000 Americans. In the auto sales and service industry, which includes the service station down the street, more than $125 billion change hands each year.

AUTOMOBILE PLANTS

The three principal "Detroit" manufacturers who also operate plants elsewhere in the United States are Chrysler, Ford, and General Motors. In addition, Japanese automakers have set up plants here and gone into cooperative manufacturing with the "big three" American companies. Emphasis in the industry has shifted to hiring higher-skilled labor. Whereas auto plants once offered good employment prospects for both high-school dropouts and graduates, today the emphasis is on at least a high school diploma or, better yet, a trade school certificate or college diploma. A recent tally of new Ford hires showed that 97 percent had high school diplomas, 4 percent had earned four-year degrees, and 33 percent had attended college. The Japanese are influencing the whole industry because their assembly line workers are chosen from top technical school graduates. As competition between manufacturers continues to heat up, education will continue to be more and more important.

In most plants you will find three major functions, each of which may employ hundreds or thousands of white- and blue-collar workers. The manufacturing department includes those who work on the never-idle assembly lines as well as numerous machines and other equipment, all concerned with producing the many items needed for each car. The engineering department has broad responsibilities not only involving designing the product with the help of specially trained artists, but also applying its skills as needed throughout the entire plant. The sales department works with the company's many dealers throughout the country who are responsible for selling the cars to the public. In addition there are those who work in administrative and specialized departments, as well as support services such as communications, purchasing, legal, financial, public relations, advertising, security, maintenance, and so forth.

If you cannot visit a plant personnel office and want to apply for a position, request an employment application from the companies for which you would like to work. Your nearest employment security office or your public library should be able to provide you with the names and addresses of principal manufacturers.

AUTOMOBILE-RELATED CAREERS

Taxicabs

"We always talked taxicabs at home. I guess it was in my blood."

Allen Kaplan leaned back in his chair and recalled his childhood, which revolved around his grandfather Baron's business. Cab Operating Company was a family affair that Sol Baron had started in the Greenpoint section of Brooklyn, New York, in 1926.

In the beginning, he bought one car and hired a driver to operate it. He was a mechanic and made certain the cab was always in good running order. After he had more cars, Fannie, his wife, became the dispatcher, telling the drivers where to go, checking their reports, and making certain they did not cheat the company. The Barons discovered that the taxi business is a seven-day-a-week, around-the-clock responsibility and is busiest at holiday times like Christmas Eve, New Year's Eve, and Easter.

When Allen was in college he considered studying law, but he decided to go into his grandfather's business instead. On the company's seventy-fifth anniversary in 1981, Cab Operating, one of the nineteen remaining fleets in New York City, owned eighty cars and enjoyed a good reputation with the Taxi and Limousine Commission, which regulates taxicabs in that metropolis.

In a city like New York, taxi regulation is strict. The number of cabs that cruise the streets, free to pick up fares on demand, is limited. Another group of cabs may respond only to telephone calls, but in Rumney, New Hampshire, a tiny town, anyone who has a car, a chauffeur's license, and proper insurance can operate a taxi service.

If this business interests you, perhaps you can start your career as a driver for a fleet of cabs or for a small company. You will probably work either the day shift, which starts anywhere between 6:00 A.M. and 8:00 A.M., or the night shift, which may begin the minute a cab arrives back at the garage between 3:00 P.M. and 5:00 P.M. As soon as the car is gassed and cleaned, you drive it out and when you return is entirely up to you as long as the car is back in time for the day shift.

Driving a taxi is an uncertain occupation. If you are in a large city you must learn where to cruise or wait for the best fares. If you live in a smaller city or town, you probably will receive your jobs at the taxi office, which takes all the taxi requests by phone. Here you must sit and wait for a call because there would be no point cruising to find business.

In some cities the job can be hazardous, especially if you must drive into high crime areas. No two days will ever be alike. Your income will depend on tips, and in addition you may receive between 40 and 50 percent of the fares you collect. It can be a long day's work, you may or may not be busy, and you could find it tiring to sit behind the wheel all that time. On the other hand, many drivers would not trade their jobs because they enjoy the freedom and the element of surprise they entail. Of the 129,000 drivers who held jobs in 1994, about four out of nine were self-employed.

Although a high school diploma may not be necessary to land a job as a taxi driver, you should have taken a driver education course and have a chauffeur's license. In some cities you may need a permit to drive as well. Check with your motor vehicle office for the requirements in your area and inquire about job prospects at the office of each taxi company.

Limousine Drivers

You may live in an area where there is a demand for chauffeurs. Unlike taxi drivers who are at the beck and call of the public, limousine chauffeurs or drivers work for one employer: a business, which has a car to drive officers and other employees to distant points; government agencies, which must provide transportation for some of their top administrators; resorts; private schools; car rental agencies, which might need you to drive cars from the rental office to the garage and back; and livery companies, which rent chauffeur-driven limousines to wealthy customers.

Some chauffeurs may be hired by people who prefer to be driven in their own cars. Other chauffeurs own their own cars, which they drive for customers who have special transportation needs.

Chauffeurs must have a chauffeur's license. They usually wear a uniform or a dark business suit and should be well mannered, attentive, and ready to render various small services and courtesies to their employers.

Service Station Employees

Although there is a growing trend toward self-service gasoline stations, even at those stations where customers fill their own tanks there must be attendants to take the money and make certain the pumps are operating satisfactorily. There are still some service stations where attendants operate the pumps, clean the windshields, and check the oil.

Such service stations also employ mechanics to repair and service cars. If a mechanic's job is interesting to you, you might start working at the gas pumps and then ask to be given assignments in the shop repairing flat tires, changing oil, lubricating, or checking brake linings. If you have the ability you might become a junior mechanic working under an experienced person. Should the station have a tow truck, you might be responsible for answering emergency calls and bringing disabled vehicles to the station.

Future employment prospects for automotive body repairers, who fix damaged cars and straighten bent bodies, are good. Every day thousands of motor vehicles are involved in traffic accidents, and most can be repaired to function and look like new. As the population increases and more cars are on the road, the need for expert repairers will increase. About 209,000 repairers were working in 1994, most of whom found employment in service stations and shops that specialized in body repairs and painting. One out of five repairers were self-employed.

Car Rental Agencies

The rack of a car rental office in a large city was jammed with reservations folders, the name of the renter written in black crayon across the top of each. Some of the names included R. Reagan, B. Bunny, L. Ronstadt, and S. Wonder. These were fake reservations used because there were not enough real customers, and the manager wanted to make it appear that the office was busy. The situation was typical of much of the industry at the beginning of the 1980s, although some of the companies, like Budget Car Rental, were doing well. Business in this industry, like many others, can fluctuate widely because much of it depends on people who travel on business or pleasure. Also when airline traffic is down, car rental activity drops off, too.

Car rental companies are found at airports, in downtown areas of cities, and in some suburbs and many small towns. At the reservation counters agents take reservations by phone or in person. These clerks fill out the necessary forms, telephone the garage for vehicles, and make certain that each customer understands the terms of the rental agreement. Drivers bring the cars from the garage and take them back when they are returned. At the garage, mechanics keep the cars in top running order while cleaners make certain they are immaculate inside and out.

A high school diploma will qualify you for simple clerical positions that may be available. Qualifications for mechanics were mentioned in the previous section, but openings for cleaners or other unskilled labor would be available on a first-come basis regardless of educational attainments.

Many high schools offer automotive repair courses as do vocational or technical schools. With this training you will be far more useful to the service station owner than the applicant who has no skills. Good mechanics are usually in demand, the work is varied and interesting, and the pay is good.

Parking Attendants

In most cities and large towns parking lots are a necessity for storing the automobiles that are driven into the crowded business districts.

Although it is estimated that 90 percent of the parking lots and garages have automatic toll collectors, there are many that hire attendants to park cars. In some large parking garages, attendants drive the cars up ramps or onto elevators, which lift them to whatever floor has parking space available.

Driving Instructors

Public schools and private driving schools employ driving instructors who teach their students while driving in dual-control training cars.

Requirements for this job vary from state to state, but you should be a high school graduate, be at least twenty-one years old, have a driver's license, and have a good driving record. Inquire at your local board of education and the offices of commercial driving schools regarding possible openings.

For further information contact International Taxicab and Livery Association, 3849 Farragut Avenue, Kensington, MD 20895; Automotive Information Council, 13505 Dulles Technology Drive, Herndon, VA 22071-3415; National Parking Association, Inc., 1112 Sixteenth Street, NW, Washington, DC 20036; or American Driver and Traffic Safety Education Association, Highway Safety Center, IUP, Indiana, PA 15705.

CHAPTER 8

AN UP-AND-DOWN BUSINESS

Over the last two thousand years, from time to time men have dreamed of somehow flying through the air. Leonardo da Vinci (1452–1519) was the first to record accurately his studies of this problem, basing his work an observations of bats, birds, and other flying creatures that soar above us. Finally balloons—lighter-than-air vehicles filled with buoyant gas—opened the door to flight. The first successful ascent took place in France during 1783, followed by many short trips thereafter in various parts of Europe. However, free-flying balloons were not the answer because they drifted according to the direction and speed of air currents and could not be steered with any reliability. The problem was solved in 1890 when a German, Count Ferdinand von Zeppelin, devised a stronger balloon and invented the first successful motor-driven airship. This led to the development of huge, highly flammable hydrogen-filled balloons to which passenger cabins and engines were attached.

In the 1920s and 1930s large zeppelins (airships named for the Count) were offering luxurious regularly scheduled service in Europe and on flights to and from North and South America. On one such trip to Lakehurst, New Jersey, the newly built *Hindenburg* caught fire at its mooring post, and the huge loss of life ended further interest in this type of travel.

Even before powered airships were perfected, many inventors were working on different types of heavier-than-air flying machines. Although several different types of aircraft were tried out in Europe toward the end of the nineteenth century, the Wright Brothers, who experimented in their Dayton bicycle shop, were the first to succeed. On December 17, 1903, they took their fragile machine, which resembled a box kite, to the beach at Kitty Hawk, North Carolina, and with Orville at the controls, Wilbur spun the propeller until the engine caught; immediately the world's first motor-powered craft carrying a human being rose and flew for twelve seconds before settling down on the sand. On the fourth flight that day, Wilbur managed to keep their airplane up for fifty-nine seconds and traveled 852 feet. Six years later the United States Army contracted for Wright airplanes, which proved the forerunner of all subsequent aircraft including today's massive jets.

A TYPICAL FLIGHT

About ninety years after the Wright Brothers' epic flight, a silvery Boeing 737 disappeared into a puffy cloud, and as it emerged into the clear the captain switched on the microphone.

"Ladies and gentlemen," said the voice. "May I have your attention, please. This is Captain Warren. We are about to start our descent from 40,000 feet and we will be landing in Boston in about twenty-five minutes. In contrast to the warm California weather that we left a short time ago, snow has been falling for about an hour, but the runway is clear and we will have no problem landing. We are estimating we will be two minutes ahead of schedule, The temperature at the airport is presently twenty degrees. For your comfort may I suggest that you remain in your seats and prepare to fasten your seat belts. Thank you."

Immediately the flight attendants started hurrying up and down the aisles, collecting the dinner trays and coffee cups. Once the dishes were stored in the galley, two of them began to take coats to the passengers, noting the seat numbers of each on tags fastened to the buttons. By the time the "Fasten Seat Belt" signs glowed, all of the clothing had been distributed and two of the flight attendants were walking slowly up the aisle checking to see that all of the passengers had fastened their belts.

"Ladies and gentlemen," the familiar voice said, "this is your captain again. We are now preparing for our final approach and landing. You may not be able to see through the snowflakes, which are falling outside, but your flight crew has a clear electronic view of our flight path. We will be on the ground in about three minutes. Thank you."

Six minutes later the plane came to a gentle stop as it nudged against the terminal dock. A moment later the cabin door opened and the first passengers departed. As soon as the cabin was empty, a crew of cleaners entered and began making it ready for the next flight.

"I'm new on this job," one of the women said to another worker. "Where does this plane go next?"

"Leaves in an hour and a half for St. Louis. Doesn't give us much time to do our job. We have to be finished within half an hour. But I'll tell you something, when a plane's late, then we *really* have to hurry. That dispatcher wants every plane cleaned on time for departure."

Meanwhile, up in the dispatcher's office, a new crew was arriving and getting ready to board the plane. The two pilots and a flight engineer were leaning over a map table and conferring with Ellen Martin, the dispatcher. She looked up and frowned.

"You're going to have some tough going, getting off the ground if this snow keeps up," she warned. "Better make sure the wings are clear; it's really coming down now."

"Don't worry, we won't take off if there's any question of safety," the older of the two pilots replied.

Meanwhile a mechanic had gone into the cockpit to check the aircraft log and see if there were any irregularities that the captain on the incoming flight had recorded. He noted the entry: "Check stabilizers—working sluggishly." The young man immediately started to check out the cables, which ran beneath the cabin floor to the rear wings and soon discovered that one of the loops through which the heavy wires passed was not properly adjusted. Other mechanics were making normal inspections while a huge fuel truck was refueling the wing tanks. The driver shivered in the storm as he held the heavy hose. A food service truck had driven up to the rear cabin door where men were removing the soiled dinner trays and dishes. Once this was done another truck arrived with the meals and beverage service for the outgoing flight.

In a departure lounge in one of the airport concourse wings that extended from the main terminal building, two passenger service representatives in trim, dark brown uniforms were standing at the desk. They were taking tickets from arriving passengers, assigning them seats, and answering their questions.

"Yes, ma'am, we expect the flight to depart on time."

"No, there should be no problem with the weather, Mr. Bain. The snowplows are clearing the runway and the snow will be removed from the wings just before takeoff. Once the plane is airborne you'll quickly rise above this weather. You should have a pleasant flight."

The pilots and the flight engineer were still studying the latest weather maps and talking with the dispatcher. "Look," she said, "there's no good weather to the west between here and Pittsburgh. Your best bet is to fly directly south to Baltimore and skirt the storm there; then go due west. See how the center of the storm is moving?" The captain nodded in agreement. "Get up to about 36,000 feet as fast as you can, and you shouldn't have any trouble."

An hour later a flight attendant swung the massive cabin door shut and locked it. The first officer switched on the engines and the plane slowly left the terminal. It turned and soon disappeared from view in the snow as it taxied to the end of the runway.

"Flight 82, get ready for takeoff," the tower operator ordered over the radio.

"Roger," the captain replied.

"Flight 82 cleared for takeoff."

The first officer applied full power and as the captain released the brakes the aircraft started down the long runway. Forty seconds later it was fully airborne and on its way to St. Louis.

To Ellen Martin, this was just one more regularly scheduled takeoff.

This account of a routine flight gives the impression that airlines always offer dependable and steady employment and that schedules go along daily without a hitch. This is not entirely true. Unlike trains, which must follow steel rails; buses and trucks, which must stay on highways; and ships, which can only sail on the water; airplanes can fly in any direction to any part of the world. Nevertheless, this freedom, as we shall see, invites unlimited competition, and that can lead to chaos.

CHANGE AND MORE CHANGE

On May 13, 1982, passengers had strapped on their seat belts and were waiting for the Braniff plane to take off when the flight attendant made an announcement.

"I have been asked to tell you that Braniff is suspending all operations." Her voice was full of emotion. "Therefore, will all passengers kindly leave the cabin. We are not going to operate this flight." The young woman turned away from the microphone and sobbed, because she, as well as some five thousand other employees, were suddenly without jobs. It was almost impossible to believe. One minute they were ready to take off for their regularly scheduled flight to Atlanta, and the next, everything had fallen apart. Without warning, there was no company, no job, no more flying.

This tragic incident is recounted not to discourage you from seeking an airline career, but to show that air transportation has its good and bad times, its advantages and drawbacks. Actually, the airlines have expanded and contracted their operations in the past like an accordion. However, in 1982, the changes were more extreme. For the first time, a major carrier had shut down altogether. At the same time, American Airlines announced that lack of business had forced it to suspend service to Columbus, Ohio, and Louisville, Kentucky, two cities it had served for over half a century. Much worse were the stories circulating that the globe-circling giant, Pan American World Airways, was in serious trouble and could become a second Braniff. Shortly thereafter the former queen of the international routes paid off its employees and sold its airplanes. Later, Eastern Air Lines disappeared into a cut-rate line thereby threatening pension and other benefits for long-time loyal employees. What was wrong? What had happened to cause these problems?

Not only had fuel costs skyrocketed, but the nation's economy had started to sag and then spun into a recession in 1981. That same year, a strike by the Professional Air Traffic Controllers Organization caused the industry great harm. The federal government fired all strikers who did not return to work by a deadline set by the President of the United States. Thereafter all airlines were forced to cut their schedules because fewer traffic controllers were manning the control towers. The airlines carried fewer passengers due to the recession and were forced to cut scheduled trips because of the controllers. This, however, was not the entire story.

From 1938 to 1978, the nation's airlines were regulated by the Civil Aeronautics Board (CAB). The CAB decided the routes each company could fly and the fares it could charge and also regulated many other aspects of the business. In 1978, Congress enacted a law that deregulated the airlines and, in effect, gave them and all newcomers the freedom to fly where they chose and to charge whatever they wished, within certain limitations.

The immediate result of this law was that many new companies sprang up giving tough competition to the older carriers and forcing them to reduce their rates and change their routes. As fares kept falling, so did profits, until most of the companies were operating in the red. Thus what had once been a generally thriving industry was now reporting one deficit after another. Employees received layoff notices, schedules were cut, services were discontinued, and airplanes were left parked at the far end of airports. One bad report followed another, but the picture was not altogether black.

Airline managements were taking a fresh look at their businesses and coming up with new ideas. One of the most important was a concept that revolutionized parts of the traditional airline route pattern. It was called "hub and spoke," which was simple and could work well for some carriers.

For example, instead of flying five planes directly from New York to Atlanta, Birmingham, Jacksonville, Mobile, and St. Petersburg, an airline would fly from New York only to Atlanta—the hub. There, other local planes—the spokes—would be scheduled for each of the other cities. The system is not as convenient for passengers because they must change planes but it reduces the number of trips and saves money. For some carriers the concept has great advantages.

Another new development brought on by deregulation has been the appearance of many small commuter airlines like Tennessee Airways, which offers much needed short-haul service along with employment opportunities. Stuart Adcock was not only Tennessee's president, principal stockholder, and head pilot, but also its chief window washer. He would pilot a flight from Nashville to Knoxville, and the instant the plane was empty he would clean the cabin, empty ashtrays, and wipe the windows.

He felt that a prerequisite for employment was a genuine enjoyment of work and the attitude that everyone did whatever work needed to be done.

The company employed forty men and women, eighteen of whom were pilots. Salaries were far below those paid elsewhere in the industry, but the company grew. Like some of the other 200 commuter lines, Adcock's had no flight attendants, served no food, and even had no toilet. He observed that deregulation produced a highly competitive atmosphere in airline operations. A success like Adcock's is bound to attract competitors, but that is what free enterprise is all about, especially under deregulation.

Since Adcock started his airline service, many of the large trunk line and transcontinental carriers have made interline arrangements with small local-service and commuter carriers. This way passengers have the convenience of making one reservation for a through trip. A newer development is for a larger company to merge the small local-service airline into its own system, so that it ultimately owns and operates both. This means that a passenger may be able to fly from one small town to another town some distance away, all on one ticket and one airline.

The really good news is that airlines provide essential transportation. Although individual companies may merge with others or even fail, planes will continue to fly. What this tells us is that if you are thinking of seeking an airline career, if possible investigate each company before approaching it for a job. Avoid the weak carriers if you can, and concentrate your job search on the stronger lines. Obviously if you live in an area served by one or two airlines you have little choice, but should you be in a large city where several carriers fly in and out of the airport, you can be a little more selective. If you know anyone who works for an airline or at an airport, talk with her or him; ask an older friend of the family who is in business to advise you, or consult one of the financial services that give up-to-date information about air transportation companies. Visit a nearby bank or a brokerage firm and explain your reason for wanting to see such reports. You should find people willing to help you.

Since airlines are here to stay, they must have people to run them, and most airlines will continue to offer good career opportunities to interested young men and women. The nature of the airline business makes it in some ways the most complicated of those in the transportation industry and, therefore, one with the greatest number of different jobs. Many jobs call for specialized training. For the purpose of reviewing the employment opportunities within the brief space available here, let's divide the business into two broad categories: airline operations and airline management. A quick visit to each area of a typical larger airline will give you an idea of some of the positions you may want to consider. All jobs mentioned here will call for at least a high school education. If additional education or training is required, that will be mentioned as well.

OPERATING THE AIRLINE

Passenger Service Personnel

The first airline employee to greet us as we arrive at the terminal is a skycap who loads our luggage on a hand cart and follows us to the ticket counter. Here the passenger service representative, a woman in a tailored blue uniform leads us to a ticket agent who examines our tickets and assigns our seats. Then the agent weighs our luggage and places it on a conveyor belt, which whisks it to the baggage room. The service representative has either received special in-service training, or was promoted from the reservations department, and is fully familiar with everything that goes on at the airport.

Ramp Service Employees

While waiting for our flight, we obtain permission to go downstairs to observe the numerous ramp service employees, those all-important men and women who perform the innumerable ground duties necessary to keep the airline flying. It is they who swarm over and through an airplane that has completed its trip and must be cleaned and serviced for its next flight. It is they who lift the baggage off the conveyor, sort it, and place it on the various carts, each marked for a different departure. They also unload baggage from incoming planes and see that it reaches the baggage claim room where passengers locate and retrieve their own luggage. It is they who load and unload mail, freight, and express. Finally, it is they who drive the food service trucks, mechanized equipment, and fuel trucks as well as assist with fueling the aircraft.

A ramp service employee, assigned to driving the various pieces of equipment, must have a driver's license and in some cases a chauffeur's license, too. Those who handle luggage, express, and freight should also be in good health and have the physical strength needed to lift heavy bags and boxes.

Mechanics

Other employees vital to airline efficiency and safety are the mechanics, who have a low profile compared to those performing ramp service duties. We see a mechanic peering up into the fuselage of a Boeing 747 while another is replacing the hydraulic line that retracts the landing gear. Airline mechanics have one or two ratings: an airframe rating (referring to the body of the airplane) or a power plant rating (referring to the engine). Most of them have both ratings, or licenses, which they obtain from the Federal Aviation Administration after successfully passing an examination. To take the test an applicant must have had at least eighteen months' experience for each license (thirty months' experience for both licenses), or have graduated from an approved aviation mechanic's training school.

You can gain this all-important license in one of three ways:

1. On-the-Job Training. A few people who have had experience in automobile repair work or other mechanical work have become aircraft mechanics by learning while working.
2. Training in the Armed Forces. Those who were aircraft mechanics in one of the military services usually have earned credit toward work experience and other requirements for the license.
3. Training in a School Certified by the Federal Aviation Administration. This is the route most men and women who hope to become airline mechanics take. The minimum amount of time required to complete the course is 1,150 hours for an airframe rating; 1,150 hours for a power plant rating; or 1,900 hours for both ratings. Before taking the FAA examination, you must prove you have had at least eighteen months' work experience for each license (thirty months' work experience for both licenses), or graduation from an approved aviation mechanic's training school. In addition you must be at least eighteen years of age and able to read, write, and speak English. For a list of approved Aviation Maintenance Technical Training Schools and information about training facilities, tuition, available financing, and other data, write: Career, Aviation Maintenance Foundation, P.O. Box 2826, Redmond, WA 98073.

Operations Office Employees

We duck into the offices that line the ramp, their large windows affording those working indoors a good view of all the aircraft as well as those employees who are servicing, repairing, or loading them. A quick walk down an aisle enables us to glance into the various offices, the first of which is that of the station manager. As the title suggests, he is the overall administrator responsible for the entire company operation at the airport. He has earned this assignment after several years spent in various positions, perhaps starting his career as an aircraft cleaner.

Flight Dispatcher

Next to his office is that of the flight dispatcher, in this case a young woman, who determines how each plane will reach its destination on time at the least operating cost, but with the maximum load of passengers and cargo. She must take into consideration such things as the temperature, the amount of fuel loaded, number of passengers booked, weight of the freight to be stowed in the cargo compartment, head winds, and weather at the plane's destination. Computers give much of this information, but it takes an alert mind to put the information together as she confers with the meteorologist and the crew of each flight regarding the best flight plan for its operation. The flight dispatcher must have a Federal Aviation Administration dispatcher's license and should have moved up from jobs such as dispatch clerk, junior flight dispatcher, radio operators meteorologist, or manager of a small station.

Schedule Coordinator

Next down the corridor is the schedule coordinator, an employee who must keep track of all aircraft and crews coming into or leaving the airport. If an airplane is delayed, he informs everyone concerned about the change. When an airplane has to be taken out of service, he must order a substitute, which may mean checking out other flights or canceling another flight if no back-up plane is available. Whenever an extra airplane is needed, the schedule coordinator must first take into consideration what servicing or maintenance may be required and whether there is enough legal flight time left for the aircraft to fly before its next regular maintenance overhaul.

But there is more to the job. A coordinator handles crew scheduling and must know who is sick, on vacation, or having a day off, as well as who has the most seniority. It is also impossible to schedule a pilot for a New York–Chicago run if that pilot has been authorized to fly only on a New York–Houston run. The schedule coordinator must have had considerable experience in the operations office before he or she is assigned to this demanding post.

Meteorologist–Radio Operator

Glancing at our watch we realize our flight will be leaving soon so we must hurry. We pass by the meteorologist who assists in plotting flight plans. He has a college degree with a major in meteorology and may even have had experience with the United States Weather Bureau or a military weather service.

In another room, loudspeakers are blaring conversations between distant airplane crews and the radio operators sitting here before microphones. These operators are always on duty ready to maintain contact with all planes in order to give and receive messages as the aircraft proceed to their destinations. These operators have had special training in technical schools and have obtained their radio operators' licenses from the Federal Communications Commission.

Food Service Jobs

At the end of the corridor, we peer through a glass door to see a huge kitchen where food is prepared for all departing flights with meal services. Here are positions with titles such as pantry worker, dishwasher, salad maker, baker, steward chef, commissary chef, chief chef, supervisor, and assistant buyer. High school graduates who can obtain a health certificate will find this a good place to start their careers in food service because if they have interest and aptitude, they will be trained and advanced on the job.

Flight Attendants

We run back upstairs to the departure lounge just in time to board our airplane. Two flight attendants greet us, show us to our seats, take our coats, and bring evening newspapers. They have been trained in the company's training school for five weeks of intensive courses on specific subjects such as routes, schedules, flight regulations, first aid, emergency procedures, good grooming, etiquette, and the proper serving of beverages and food. After graduation, the first assignments are usually to fill in on extra flights or substitute for those on vacation or sick leave. Later, assignments are made on the basis of seniority, so that experienced attendants have their choices of flights and times. Advancement is probably limited to becoming a flight service instructor in the training school, a passenger service representative, receptionist, or recruiting representative in the personnel department.

Flight Crew

Once our aircraft is airborne we are invited to visit the cockpit and meet the crew. The captain sits on the left-hand seat in front of the instrument panel, which displays a confusing array of gauges, dials, levers, and buttons. To the captain's right is the first officer. Behind, in a little recess, the walls of which resemble the instrument panel, is the ever-watchful flight engineer who constantly is alert for any signs of malfunctioning equipment and who also has certain duties that involve adjusting and operating various equipment.

New airline pilots usually start as flight engineers. Although airlines prefer an applicant who has a flight engineer's license, they may train a new employee who has only a commercial pilot's license.

"What are the requirements for becoming a pilot?" we asked the captain as he relaxed for a moment, the first officer having taken over the controls.

"You must be at least eighteen and a high school graduate, but most airlines require two years of college and prefer college graduates," he replied. "You must be able to pass a strict physical exam, have 20/20 vision with or without glasses, and have good hearing. You must pass a written test, which includes questions on the principles of safe flight, navigation techniques, and FAA regulations. Of course, you must be able to demonstrate your flying ability to the FAA examiner."

The captain smiled and turned in his seat. "That's not all. Pilots who are going to fly in bad weather must be licensed by the FAA to fly by instruments. This calls for forty hours of experience in instrument flying, passing a written examination, and demonstrating your ability in instrument flying." He paused to point at himself. "Those of us who are captains also have to obtain an airline transport pilot's license. To get this piece of paper, you have to be at least twenty-three and have a minimum of fifteen hundred hours of flying experience in both night and instrument flying."

"Very interesting," we observed, "but where does one learn to fly?"

"I believe that the FAA has now certified some fourteen hundred civilian flying schools, including a few colleges and universities that offer degree credit for pilot training. It's also possible to learn for nothing by joining one of the military services where you can gain considerable jet experience. I'd advise any young person interested in sitting up here in the cockpit to get a college education first, and then a pilot's license and a flight engineer's license. This is one business in which you can't be over-qualified!"

A *List of Certified Pilot Schools* may be obtained by writing the Superintendent of Documents, Government Printing Office, Washington, DC 20402. For further information on airline pilots write the Airline Pilots Association, 1625 Massachusetts Avenue, NW, Washington, DC 20036.

If you have ever wondered whether women can qualify as airline pilots, read on. In May 1987, when American Airlines' Flight 417 taxied away from Washington's National Airport bound for Dallas/Fort Worth and Oklahoma City, all three pilots on the flight deck and all four flight attendants in the passenger cabins of the Boeing 727 stretch plane were women. For Captain Beverley Bass, it was her second claim to fame. Just a few weeks earlier, she had become American's first woman captain.

Now we are back in the cabin; our seat belts are fastened. As the plane makes the final approach for landing we pass over the company's flight attendants training school and flight training academy near the airport. The flight instructors have had airline experience plus some teaching experience, which qualifies them to teach new flight crew members and to check them periodically once they have started working.

"Please remain in your seats until the seat belt sign has been turned off," the flight attendant requests. A few minutes later we are walking through the passenger terminal heading for the limousine to take us downtown where the company's headquarters is located.

AIRLINE MANAGEMENT

In contrast to the hubbub at the airport, the six floors of dignified offices high in a city skyscraper at first seem almost uninteresting, if not dull. The impression is erroneous, though, for the more we learn about what goes on within these walls, which are so remote from the airplanes, the more fascinating it all becomes.

The Reservations Department

Our first stop is in the reservations department. Here, all of the incoming telephone calls requesting information or reservations are received by numerous reservations agents, each of whom works within a tiny cubicle. Apart from a headset, a copy of the company's schedules and tariffs, and the *Official Airline Guide,* which contains schedules of all the airlines, the only other equipment in the cubicle is the computer terminal. This is connected to the reservations computer center, which is located in another city 600 miles away.

The computer is really an electronic brain with a fantastic memory. When a passenger requests a seat on a certain flight, the agent asks the computer if there is space on that particular flight. The answer is flashed back instantly. Then the agent is able to make the reservation by typing the date, flight number, destination, and the passenger's name, address, and telephone number. This information is stored in the computer. Later it will be retrieved when it is time to see how many passengers are booked for that flight and a passenger manifest is prepared.

The reservations department or the ticket counter are two of the best places to start one's airline career. Usually a week or ten days' classroom instruction in routings and fares is followed by three weeks of on-the-job training. Then, the agent is considered ready to work independently. The knowledge and experience gained in these positions give one an invaluable background for future advancement.

Sales Positions

The reservations department is part of the general sales department, which is located on the floor above. Although airlines depend for the most part on their newspaper, magazine, radio, and TV advertising as well as on the thousands of travel agents for their customers, a number of specialists are needed to handle various sales functions.

Walking through the corridors, we are able to get a good idea of the range of sales activities by looking at the names of the different divisions that we pass:

- Passenger Sales Division. Responsible for planning and carrying out sales programs.
- Freight Sales Division. Same as above, but for freight.
- Reservations and Ticket Offices Division. Oversees the operation of all reservations and ticket offices, planning and opening new offices, and training new employees.
- Interline Sales Division. Encourages other airlines to route as much business as possible on each other's planes.
- Agency Sales Division. Plans programs designed to increase the cooperation of travel agencies in booking business with the airline.
- Convention Sales Division. Contacts organizations that will be holding large conventions and persuades convention delegates to use the airline.
- Tariff Division. Computes and publishes all of the company's fares and freight tariffs.
- Schedule Division. Prepares and publishes all the schedules for both the passenger planes and airfreighters that the company will operate.
- Advertising Division. Prepares and places all company advertising.

While talking with one of the sales executives we asked how one prepares for a position in the sales department.

"Many of our people have transferred from the reservations and ticket offices division," he said. "On the other hand, we hire college graduates who have backgrounds in transportation, economics, statistics, business administration, or computer operation, and I find that they learn quickly and become very satisfactory employees."

Public Relations and Purchasing

Taking the elevator to the next floor, as we continue our tour of the headquarters building, we come to the public relations department. Its mission is to provide the public with information about the company, at the same time promoting the company's image. Whenever an airline has a problem newsworthy enough to make the TV newscast or headlines, it is the job of the public relations department to see that it receives sympathetic treatment.

"All of our staff are devoted to just one purpose," the public relations director told us, "and that is telling the outside world about our airline and how great it is. But when we have a serious accident, we pull hard on the reversing lever and all our efforts are bent on toning down the news reports and trying to see that the TV, radio, and newspapers are factual in their reporting and free of sensationalism."

To our query regarding job opportunities in his department the executive replied: "Apart from the clerical positions, we like to hire men and women from schools that specialize in public relations or journalism. Sometimes we take a man or woman who has a newspaper background."

The much larger purchasing department is across the hall. Here we learn that millions of dollars are spent annually by staff members as they buy everything from paper clips to multimillion dollar airplanes. Most of the buying is done by purchasing agents or buyers with new employees being assigned to work with a senior member of the department. College degrees are necessary for good positions, and beginning jobs require that you have at least taken an associate degree program in purchasing.

The Finance Department

Occupying an entire floor, the sprawling finance department somehow reminds us of a bank. Its large area is filled with rows of desks at which men and women are working industriously. Here auditors, statisticians, financial analysts, economists, clerks, section and department heads are busy trying to keep track of the $1.5 million that flow in and out of the office each day from the innumerable ticket offices and freight depots.

The two most important sections of any airline finance department are *revenue accounting,* which keeps track of all incoming money, and *disbursements,* which pays all the bills. Closely associated with disbursements is the payroll section, responsible for preparing thousands of weekly and bi-weekly pay checks. We pause at the next section to chat briefly with the manager of the insurance department. Her staff is concerned with handling every type of insurance from the multimillion dollar coverage on the aircraft fleet and passengers to the group life or health insurance, which is available to all employees.

Moving along the aisle, we find a group of employees who are familiar with both accounting procedures and tax laws. They staff the tax section, which houses an increasingly important group of specialists, because federal income taxes alone can run into the millions of dollars. Other taxes are collected by cities, counties, and states where the company's planes touch down.

The budget section crammed into one corner of the floor is most influential because these employees forecast income and expenses for the years ahead. They also review every departmental budget to make certain it is not too large in proportion to company assets.

Every section has its typists, secretaries, and accounting clerks, often called bookkeeping clerks, who have taken accounting or bookkeeping courses in school. They perform a wide variety of duties, mostly of a routine nature. The other more specialized positions call for men and women who have had college courses in economics, statistics, mathematics, or business administration. Those employees who have done graduate work or attended a business school qualify for the more responsible posts, many of which lead to top management positions.

Other Home Office Departments

It has been a long day and now we conclude our tour by walking quickly through the remaining departments before everyone leaves at five o'clock.

Airlines own little or no property. They lease their office space and rent hangars as well as all of the lobbies, concourses, ticket counter areas, and offices at airport terminals. Planning and supervising construction of hangars, ticket counters, office and other space, negotiating leases, and working closely with airport managements are the responsibilities of the properties department.

In the personnel department we see men and women busy interviewing and hiring applicants for jobs, keeping all of the personnel records, setting wage and salary scales, negotiating contracts with labor unions, and handling employee benefits.

Finally, after we pass the legal department, we stop at the door to the mail room. Here a number of young men and women are busy sorting and stamping mail, wrapping packages, and packing mail sacks for delivery to the post office. This is an ideal place for those just out of high school to start. Many an airline executive began his or her career sorting and delivering mail.

With a farewell wave to the receptionist we step into an elevator and go quickly to the ground floor. We have had an interesting day observing the operations of an airline that offers a great variety of career opportunities in the transportation industry.

FINDING YOUR JOB

If you live in a city served by several airlines, watch the help-wanted newspaper advertisements. In addition, apply at the personnel offices of those companies that offer the best opportunities for immediate employment and advancement. Should you live where there is no airline service or where only one or two carriers offer limited schedules, you must try a different approach. Check with your state employment security office to see what airline job listings, if any, it might have. If nothing is available, be sure to ask the interviewer for any suggestions. Bear in mind that these specialists keep up to date on employment trends.

Write the personnel department of those airlines where you think you would like to work. You can obtain the names and addresses of all airlines by consulting the *World Aviation Directory,* published by the Ziff-Davis Publishing Company, or by obtaining a list of certificated airlines from the Air Transport Association of America.

If you know anyone who works for an airline or has a friend employed by one of the carriers, talk with him or her to obtain firsthand information. If possible, secure the name of someone in the personnel department whom you might contact directly by mail or in person.

Further information about the air transport industry may be obtained by writing the Air Transport Association of America, 1301 Pennsylvania Avenue, NW, Washington, DC 20006; or one or more of the unions of airline workers (see Appendix B). A companion VGM Career Horizons book, *Opportunities in Airline Careers,* gives extensive information about the airlines and the careers they offer.

A FINAL WORD

Even as late as 1996 various news items might have given you the impression that the airlines were in trouble. Airports were overcrowded, a number of near mid-air collisions had been reported, there were delays in dispatching flights, and there were extremely confusing fare structures. Worse of all there had been two bad accidents, which raised serious safety problems.

"What kind of industry is this for a lifetime career?" You might well ask.

We offer four reasons for considering aviation in your future plans:

1. Both the government and the airlines recognized the problems and were doing their best to correct them. Such chaos has occurred before and has been rectified, as it will be again.
2. All types of transportation will undoubtedly experience accidents. From 1980–1995 the same number of people died each year in air

crashes as were struck by lightning. Your chances of dying in a car or taxi are thirty-seven times greater each mile than on an airplane.
3. The nation's economy depends on continued airline operations. A visit to any busy airport will confirm this if you watch the planes loading and unloading not only streams of passengers, but also tons of express, mail, and freight.
4. After spending over twenty-five years in the industry, the author has every confidence that aviation offers even greater opportunities than it did during the so-called expansion years.

Safe and inexpensive air travel is one of our nation's greatest achievements. The industry is constantly striving to better its record. That's why you can depend on it; there can be a future in this challenging industry for you, too.

CHAPTER 9

TRAVEL AGENTS GO PLACES

Travel agencies are by no means as new as might be expected. As early as 1841 an Englishman, Thomas Cook, planned the first guided tours for small parties. In 1852 he publicly advertised "Cook's Tours" to attract tourists eager to travel abroad. Twenty years later a travel agency opened in the United States, and from that small start a large industry took root and grew to some 20,000 professional consultants.

Today travel agents not only secure bus, cruise, plane, and train tickets as well as reservations for rental cars and hotel rooms, but also act as travel consultants and travel salespersons. Some even organize their own tours and act as tour guides or book their clients on tours conducted by other organizations. Four of the largest are AAA (American Automobile Association), American Express, Carlson/Wagonlit Travel, and Thomas Cook & Son.

What makes the job of travel agent one of the most difficult in the transportation business is the never-ending confusion surrounding airline schedules and fares. At one time it was said that an agent could compute as many as twenty different fares between Boston and Washington, depending on the carrier, type of service, time of day, day of the week, length of stay in Washington, type of equipment flown, and age of the passenger or relationship to the purchaser of the tickets.

To set up a client's long journey with numerous stopovers may require calls to several carriers for the latest information on schedules and fares. Most travel agencies have computer terminals tied into airline reservations systems, and they are a great help for obtaining information and confirming reservations on any carrier. But to be a successful travel agent calls for a real knowledge of the business.

If you have patience and can stand pressure, this could become an interesting career. Generally speaking, the pay is not what it might be considering the long hours and hard work, but there is one good fringe benefit—free "educational trips" that airlines and hotels offer, hoping you will refer business to them once you are familiar with their service.

Today automation in the form of the new electronic ticket machines (ETMs) threaten many travel agents just as they do bank tellers. By telephoning an airline, bus company, or Amtrak, one can make travel arrangements and at the nearest ETM pay for and obtain the tickets. Obviously this may eliminate some travel agencies, but if one needs help in deciding where to go and stay, no ETM will substitute for a knowledgeable man or woman. Another problem for the industry is that many airlines have reduced the traditional commissions paid travel agents for handling reservations and issuing tickets. Although the workload is no less, the greatly reduced commissions do not, in many cases, provide enough income to pay for the required staff. We mention these developments because they probably will cut employment in this field somewhat but need not affect your career plans if you are serious about wanting to enter this industry.

Private employment agencies and your state employment security office are the best places to find out about the possible openings in travel agencies as well as any large corporation that uses an employee rather than a travel agent to make all company travel arrangements. If you obtain no leads, contact the agencies yourself to see if any of them could use a beginner who is eager to learn the business. A high school diploma is a must for a travel agent, and general familiarity with airline, Amtrak, and bus routes is essential. Some technical schools offer two-year programs in travel and tourism, and a few colleges offer bachelor's and master's degrees in this subject. The American Society of Travel Agents offers a correspondence course that provides a basic understanding of the industry. Fluency in a foreign language can be helpful when applying for a position.

For further information contact the American Society of Travel Agents at 1701 King Street, Alexandria, VA 22314, or Travel Industry Association of America, 1133-21 Street, NW, Washington, DC 20036.

CHAPTER 10

DON'T OVERLOOK TERMINALS!

No doubt the first transportation terminals served a railroad and consisted of shelters erected at each end of a short railroad line. Terminals as we think of them today are stations that serve as a junction between two or more carriers. During the 1800s as more railroads were built and met other roads where they could exchange passengers and freight, terminals grew in importance and size until most large cities serviced by several roads boasted imposing structures that offered many amenities.

Without a doubt Grand Central Terminal in New York City became the most famous. Its huge concourse marked by the star-studded ceiling above and the famous, round, shiny information booth below; its spacious hallways extending out in every direction to connect with office buildings, hotels, and stores; and its countless shops and restaurants have made it a landmark. It has been said that a person could live in a hotel with an underground entrance to Grand Central and obtain everything he or she needed without ever going outdoors.

Today other large sprawling terminals at major airports offer a wide variety of services and stores. One can walk seemingly forever from one end to the other of Chicago's O'Hare Airport terminal, while in other large and newer terminals, connecting airline passengers ride in people movers or monorail trains.

TODAY'S TERMINALS

Any weekday at five o'clock visit Seattle's ferry terminal, one of Chicago's commuter railroad terminals, or the mammoth New York Port Authority Bus Terminal. As you watch the thousands of men and women rushing to catch ferries, planes, trains, or buses, you will realize what important places terminals can be. Even the small terminal in Vermont's White River Junction, which serves Greyhound and Vermont Transit buses, can be a hectic place as frantic passengers run up to the single window for tickets or information and the loudspeaker blares "Last call for New York City on platform three." The difference between this terminal and the one in New York is a matter of size, but the operations and problems are similar.

What is a modern terminal? Simply stated it is a place from which passengers, freight, and express depart and arrive. Whatever form of transportation it may serve, a terminal must supply facilities for loading and unloading passengers and freight, and in the case of a passenger terminal, provide waiting rooms, restaurant and comfort facilities, as well as ready access to ground transportation. In addition it should be possible to fuel, clean, provision, and repair the planes, trains, vehicles, or ships. Thus a wide range of workers is needed to provide all the services required.

The organization and management of terminals vary widely. At a large airport each airline may have its own terminal, which is part of the overall complex. At a small airport the terminal may serve two or three airlines but have a consolidated ticket office with baggage handlers, mechanics, and fleet service workers. These workers are employees of the terminal company. Some bus terminals offer consolidated services with two or more lines using the facilities. In the case of railroads or ferries, where usually only one carrier arrives and departs, one group of employees provides all the necessary services.

Whatever the arrangements, they are of little consequence to you if you are investigating career possibilities at a terminal. However, you should bear in mind that if you are a mechanic, for example, you might find that the terminal management has no such job openings because each of the carriers uses its own employees. On the other hand, were you interested in a reservations or ticketing position, you might learn that the terminal company provides these services to all the carriers, and it is the place to apply. The best way to discover what job openings there are is to visit the terminal's personnel office.

We have already covered the career opportunities available with each of the major forms of transportation. As for terminals, regardless of who owns or manages them, they all must maintain grounds and roads; do maintenance for which carpenters, electricians, plumbers, painters, and other craftsworkers are required; and provide security and clerical functions. There is also opportunity for unskilled laborers, typists, accountants, and computer specialists.

In large terminals there is a need for a public relations staff, specialists in personnel, planners, and purchasing agents. The top positions would be those of manager and assistant manager, posts for which several years of experience are required.

Most terminals rent space to concessions: restaurants, newsstands, car rental agencies, gift shops, and in large city terminals, stores of all kinds. Working in a restaurant or store would provide temporary employment and give you an opportunity to check for other openings in the field you want to enter.

The VGM Career Horizons book, *Opportunities in Airline Careers,* contains a chapter on airports, and it touches on job opportunities at airport terminals.

TRAVELER'S AID

In most large terminals you will find a desk in or near the waiting room where arriving travelers can easily spot it and its sign: "Traveler's Aid Society." These services date back to 1851 when the mayor of St. Louis saw the need to help travelers headed west who were stranded in the city. He paid to set up a service to help those who were penniless, homeless, starving, lost, or in need of a job or counseling.

Today more than ninety agencies in the United States, Canada, and Puerto Rico have paid staffs and volunteers to help the two and a half million men and women—who include runaway juveniles and immigrants as well as the unemployed, sick, disabled, homeless, disoriented, and stranded traveler—who seek help each year. Even though today some 90 percent of all travelers use their automobiles, local traveler's aid societies are finding increasing numbers of motorists coming to them from the highways to obtain help of one kind or another.

If interested, talk with the representatives in your city, or contact the National Organization of Traveler's Aid Societies, 512 C Street, NW, Washington, DC 20002.

CHAPTER 11

WORKING FOR UNCLE SAM

Do you know who is the largest employer in the United States, if not the world? The answer is the federal government. Then there are also the state, county, and municipal governments, to say nothing of the many public authorities, some of which operate transportation systems. Altogether, the number of men and women working for the government totals somewhere between 3.5 and 4 million. Of course transportation-related jobs are not numerous in the state, county, and municipal categories, and therefore, you will find your best opportunities probably exist in U.S. worldwide operations.

Even though the 1990s ushered in a cutback in government expenditures and reduction in the number of government employees, certain functions must continue. The military received additional billions while other government services were cut. The armed forces are the best place to start our survey of jobs because although we have a military establishment made up of volunteers, the door is wide open to young men and women who can qualify for admission. What makes military service so attractive is the opportunity to obtain vocational training. At a time when education is expensive and beyond the reach of many, it makes sense to investigate a career with one of the military services.

A word of caution here: whereas previously many high school graduates and others looked upon the military as a last resort employer, this no longer is true. All the armed services are much more difficult to enter than they were previously. A good education is a big plus because almost 94 percent of the new recruits are high school graduates and nearly all of the balance have earned high school equivalency certificates. "Be mentally, morally, and physically qualified," a recruiting officer advised those interested in applying to one of the services.

THE ARMED FORCES

The four principal military services, Air Force, Army, Marines (actually a branch of the Navy), and the Navy, offer a wide range of career opportunities in clerical and administrative work, electrical and electronic occupations, and hundreds of other specialties, many of which are related to transportation.

Transportation is essential to all of the services. You may enlist in any one of a variety of programs that involve different combinations of active or reserve duty. Job training available to enlisted personnel may depend on the length of service commitment, general and technical aptitudes, personal preferences, and most of all, the needs of the service at that time.

It would be impossible to list all the career opportunities available in the various services. The following list is typical of transportation skills that are transferable to civilian positions if you should decide to resign from the service after completing your enlistment. The numeral that follows each listing indicates the number of weeks training is required. You should bear in mind that the technological changes and needs of each service vary from time to time, hence courses that you might have hoped to take can be dropped or altered.

Aircraft Maintenance: Aviation Maintenance Administration (7), Aviation Safety Equipment (9), Aviation Structure Mechanic (9), Aviation Hydraulic Mechanic (7), Basic Helicopter Course (6).

Air Traffic Control & Enlisted Flight Crews: Aerial Navigator (26), Airborne Radio Operator (16), Air Traffic Controller (8).

Avionics: Avionics Technician (12), Advanced First Term Avionics (26), Aviation Electrician Mate (11), Precision Measuring Equipment Technician (3), Avionics Technician Intermediate (28).

Electronics Maintenance: Aviation Radio Technician (9), Aviation Radio Repairer (20), Meteorological Equipment Maintenance (18), Aviation Radar Technician (17), Ground Radar Technician (27), Aviation Fire Control Technician (7).

Motor Transport: Fuels and Electrical Systems Repair (11), Basic Automotive Mechanic (12), Metal Body Repair (8), Advanced Automotive Mechanic (16).

Transportation: Defense Advanced Traffic Management (3), Installation Traffic Management (4).

There are many excellent benefits for those serving in the armed forces. For example, you may earn thirty days vacation a year, obtain very inexpensive life insurance, have low-cost dental and medical care, and you may visit the commissary and post exchange where you can do your shopping and find year-round bargain prices. Best of all, you can retire after twenty years of service with a generous pension.

Don't ignore the army as a possible means of entering the transportation field. It operates its own airline, its own traffic control system, and, of course, motorized equipment of all kinds.

Each of the services publishes pamphlets that describe entrance requirements, training and advancement opportunities, and other aspects of military life. These publications are available at all recruiting stations, most state employment security offices, and in high schools, colleges, and public libraries. Consult your telephone book for the nearest recruiting office, which will be listed under "United States Government," or write the following:

U.S. Army Recruiting Command, Fort Sheridan, IL 60037.

Director of Public Affairs, Department of the Air Force, 1670 Air Force, Pentagon, Washington, DC 20330-1670.

Director, Personnel Procurement Division, Headquarters, U.S. Marine Corps, Washington, DC 20380.

Office of Information, Department of the Navy, Washington, DC 20350.

Information Office, U.S. Coast Guard, 2100 Second Street, SW, Washington, DC 20593.

THE NAVY MILITARY SEALIFT COMMAND

One unusual branch of the service is the Navy's Military Sealift Command, which employs civilians both ashore and at sea.

MSC has a variety of positions on its ships, such as those for licensed steam and diesel engineers, licensed deck officers, radio officers, deck and refrigeration engineers, able seamen, oilers and firemen-watertenders, electricians and machinists, yeoman-storekeepers, and cooks and bakers. Competition is keen for most positions; however, the greater the skill an applicant has, the better the chances for employment. On shore the MSC utilizes naval architects, marine engineers, marine transportation specialists, and computer specialists.

Applicants for positions at sea must have the appropriate U.S. Coast Guard Merchant Marine documents or validated documents with the necessary endorsement. For further information write Office of Information, Department of the Navy, Washington, DC 20350.

UNITED STATES CUSTOMS SERVICE

The customs service was one of the first government agencies created in 1789, its purpose being to assess and collect the revenue on imported merchandise and to enforce customs and related laws. Today it has some 14,000 employees, most of whom are located at the nearly 300 ports of entry. A few are assigned to overseas posts.

The customs service enforces its own as well as approximately 400 laws and regulations for 40 other federal agencies. It also conducts a variety of antismuggling programs.

Although this work has nothing to do with the actual transporting of people or goods, it is, nevertheless, an essential part of our transportation system in that travel and shipping of goods to the United States are involved.

Here are brief descriptions of the principal career positions with the service.

Customs inspectors are probably the only customs employees with whom the public is familiar. At airports and other ports of entry, they inspect your baggage to ensure compliance with the tariff laws and try to detect smugglers.

Inspectors review ship and plane manifests as they examine cargo and control shipments that are transferred under bond to ports throughout the United States. Customs inspectors are the nation's front-line defenders against smuggling as they work in cooperation with customs special agents, patrol officers, and import specialists, as well as the FBI and the Drug Enforcement Administration. As part of the law enforcement team, inspectors perform personal searches, seize contraband, and apprehend violators. They may also be required to wear side arms.

Special agents comprise a highly trained investigative force of the service whose purpose is to frustrate the efforts of smugglers. Aided by complex radio communications networks, which provide critical data on the activities of suspects, they follow the journey of contraband from its entry along our borders and coastlines. Special agents are assigned to duty stations in most ports of entry and may be called on to travel during the course of their work.

Customs patrol officers carry out the difficult task of detecting and apprehending violators of the 400 statutes enforced by the service. They prevent smuggling into the country and may serve anywhere in the United States from along the frozen northern border to the deserts of the southwest, from urban waterfronts to secluded coastlines. No two assignments are alike; nor are any two working days.

Import specialists assess the rate of duties, an activity that makes the service a major revenue-producing agency of the government. They examine import entry documents, check to see that the imported merchandise agrees with the description, and then classify the merchandise under the tariff schedules to determine the correct duty required. Import specialists become experts in one or more lines of merchandise, and in order to make sure that their expertise remains current, they often examine selected shipments.

Customs aids perform semitechnical duties that require a specialized knowledge of provisions of customs laws and regulations. They assist inspectors and other specialists in the service.

There are other interesting career possibilities, too.

Canine enforcement officers train and use dogs to enforce customs laws pertaining to the smuggling of marijuana, narcotics, and dangerous drugs.

Customs pilots are part of a program of air surveillance of illegal traffic crossing U.S. borders by air, land, or sea. Pilots also apprehend, arrest, and search violators of customs and related laws.

Customs chemists play an important part in protecting the nation's health and safety as well as the security of the country's commerce. They are called upon to analyze imported merchandise ranging from textile fibers to contraband narcotics.

In addition to the above specialist positions there are numerous data processing positions in the Washington headquarters, to say nothing of the usual clerical openings.

Customs jobs are filled and administered under the competitive civil service system. Since the educational and experience requirements for each of the jobs vary, it is best to check with the nearest Federal Job Information Center or the Customs Service itself to learn about openings and what the requirements are for each.

For further information write the United States Customs Service, Headquarters Personnel Branch, 1301 Constitution Avenue, NW, Washington, DC 20229.

AIR TRAFFIC CONTROL

On August 3, 1980, federal air traffic controllers began a nationwide strike that was declared illegal. Their union had rejected a final offer for a new contract, but in spite of the walkout about 60 percent of the 14,200 scheduled daily airline flights continued to operate. Supervisors and nonstrikers manned the radar-operated control towers.

President Reagan warned the strikers that unless they returned to work by 11:00 A.M. on August 5, they would be immediately fired. After most of the 13,000 controllers refused to report to their towers, the Federal Aviation Administration sent out the first of the dismissal notices. Although controllers in some other countries refused to clear departures of flights to the United States, this action fizzled as President Reagan remained adamant in his stand against the strikers. Military controllers and supervisors continued to handle the towers with those controllers who had not gone on strike. All airline flight schedules were cut back and a long-range program was instituted for hiring and training controllers. In 1982 the union announced plans to disband. A new union was later formed to represent the controllers who by 1996 numbered 23,000.

Although it announced in 1987 that it would be hiring 2,000 additional controllers, the Federal Aviation Administration, which is in charge of all air traffic control activities, has not let down its standards. Here is how the administration defines the required background:

"General Experience: Progressively responsible experience in administrative, technical, or other work, which demonstrated potential for learning and performing air traffic control work.

"Specialized Experience: Experience in a military or civilian air traffic facility, which demonstrated possession of the knowledge, skills, and abilities required to perform the level of work of the specialization for which application is made."

It may be possible to substitute certain education and flight training for experience. But you must check with the Federal Aviation Administration regarding current qualifications. In any case, you must pass a physical examination that includes tests for color vision, a comprehensive written test, and you must be interviewed. The maximum age of thirty was established for entry into a tower, but this requirement may be changed.

Controllers normally work a forty-hour week in FAA control towers at airports using radio, radar, electronic computers, telephones, traffic control lights, and other devices for communication. Night and weekend hours are rotated.

Controllers give taxiing instructions to aircraft on the ground, takeoff instructions, and clearances to incoming planes. At busy locations these duties are rotated among staff members about every two hours. A controller must work quickly, and demands increase as the traffic mounts, especially when there are poor flying conditions and traffic backs up. Brief rest periods provide some relief but they are not always possible. Shift work is necessary in this occupation.

The FAA employs controllers at more than four hundred airports. A few towers are located outside the continental United States in Alaska, Hawaii, Puerto Rico, the Virgin Islands, and American Samoa.

Promotion from trainee to a higher grade professional controller depends on satisfactory progression in the training program. Trainees who do not successfully complete the training courses are terminated or reassigned to other positions.

During the first year a trainee is on probation, but afterwards he or she may advance from positions backing up professional controllers to primary positions of responsibility. It takes a controller from three to six years of experience to reach peak performance.

Some professional controllers are selected for research activities with FAA's National Aviation Facilities Experimental Center in Atlantic City, New Jersey. Others may serve as instructors. Trainees receive from fifteen to nineteen weeks of instruction at the FAA Academy in Oklahoma City, Oklahoma, and then are assigned to a tower for on-the-job training under close supervision.

Additional information about air traffic control is contained in the VGM Career Horizons *Opportunities in Airline Careers.* For further information about employment opportunities, contact the Office of Communications, Office of Personnel Management, 1900 E Street, SW, Washington, DC 20415-0001.

FEDERAL REGULATORY AGENCIES

Recently there has been a trend in the federal government to deregulate. The Civil Aeronautics Board, for example, disbanded in 1984.

It should be noted that many of the positions in the federal agencies concerned with transportation call for specialists in the fields of accounting, data processing, engineering, finance, highway traffic, personnel, planning, research, safety, and transportation. In addition, there are the usual office support positions in the clerical areas.

For information about current job openings contact your nearest state employment security office or the U.S. Office of Personnel Management (see above for address).

Department of Transportation

This agency establishes the nation's transportation policy. Under its umbrella there are ten administrations. Their jurisdictions include highway planning, development, and construction; urban mass transit; railroads; aviation; and the safety of waterways, ports, highways, and oil and gas pipelines. Decisions made by this department, in conjunction with the appropriate state and local officials, strongly affect other programs, such as land planning, energy conservation, scarce resource utilization, and technological change.

One of the agencies under the Department of Transportation is the United States Coast Guard. It maintains a system of rescue vessels, aircraft, and communications facilities to carry out its function of saving life and property on the high seas and navigable waters of the United States.

For further information about the Department of Transportation contact the Office of Public Affairs (DOT) Information Center, 400 Seventh Street, SW, Washington, DC 20590.

Federal Maritime Commission

This commission regulates the waterborne foreign and domestic offshore commerce of the country. It ensures that United States international trade is open to all nations on fair and equitable terms and protects against unauthorized activity in the waterborne commerce of the United States.

For further information contact the Office of Congressional and Public Affairs, Maritime Commission, 400 Seventh Street, SW, Washington, DC 20590.

National Highway Traffic Administration

This agency seeks to ensure that all types of transportation in the United States are conducted safely. The board investigates accidents, conducts studies, and makes recommendations to government agencies. It also regulates the procedures for reporting accidents and promotes the safe transport of hazardous materials by government and private industry.

For further information contact the Office of Public and Consumer Affairs, National Highway Traffic Administration, 400 Seventh Street, SW, Washington, DC 20590.

STATE AND LOCAL REGULATORY AGENCIES

Another layer of agencies regulating intrastate transportation will be found in each of the states. They have various names, the most usual being the Public Utilities Commission, although you may find Department of Transportation or even Railroad Commission. Since their jurisdictions are limited to operations within the state, most of them offer limited career opportunities. You can obtain the name and address of your state agency from your public library or by writing to the secretary of state at your state capital. You may find openings for drivers and mechanics with your state highway department. Contact your nearest state employment security office or the state civil service commission for information about current job openings.

In some of the larger municipalities you may find agencies that regulate taxi and limousine service within the city borders, or the operation of the transit system. There may be an agency that provides automobiles and drivers to transport municipal employees on official business. As in the case of the state, the highway department may offer job opportunities for drivers, mechanics, and other job assignments. Consult your telephone book under the listing for your city for the proper name of such agencies, or visit the civil service commission.

CHAPTER 12

YOUR NEXT STEP

By now you have seen that transportation, like other industries, offers both advantages and disadvantages. It might be helpful to enumerate them.

ADVANTAGES

Since transportation is as essential to the nation as agriculture, you will experience a higher degree of job security working in it than in many other businesses. Unlike some industries that may lay off many employees or close down altogether during economic recessions, a carrier may be forced to retrench somewhat, but not to the extent that many harder-hit firms might.

If you like to travel, you may find a position that will enable you to do so. Even though you hold a desk job in an airline, bus, or rail company, you may enjoy free travel privileges along with other fringe benefits. Best of all, this business has glamour because travel can be stimulating and fun.

DISADVANTAGES

On the other hand, transportation is a seven-day-a-week, around-the-clock business. This means you may be assigned to work the night shift (4:00 P.M. to midnight) or the graveyard shift (midnight to 8:00 A.M.), to say nothing of Saturdays, Sundays, and holidays. Furthermore, if your job involves working on buses, planes, trains, ships, trucks, or other vehicles that travel long distances, you may be away from home a lot. Because air, marine, and ground transport runs year-round in every kind of weather, you can anticipate encountering all types of weather conditions and occasionally dangerous travel conditions.

EDUCATIONAL TRAINING

After finishing this book, if you think a career in transportation is for you, learn all you can about that branch of the industry and the jobs that interest you. Find out what education or specialized training is required, so that you can start preparing yourself as soon as possible. Discuss your ideas with other people whose judgment you respect, or preferably, someone in the industry.

To summarize what has been said before, transportation jobs require one of four levels of educational training:

1. High school for unskilled entry positions, such as cleaners, custodians, food handlers, mailroom clerks, and drivers.
2. Technical or vocational school for mechanics, secretaries, bookkeepers, pilots, and seamen.
3. Undergraduate degree for many entry positions in supervisory or professional positions.
4. Graduate degree principally for professionals, such as engineers, lawyers, librarians, computer specialists, management specialists, and public relations practitioners.

The importance of acquiring computer skills cannot be overemphasized. As an example, if you apply at the Case Corporation (manufacturer of farm machinery) for a white-collar position, you will not be considered unless you are computer literate.

Regardless of the educational requirements of the job you are contemplating, start today to chart your future so that you can make it happen. Lack of money need not discourage you or keep you from pursuing a career that calls for technical or college training. It is quite possible you can obtain a scholarship, loan, or grant; earn some of the money while you are studying; or find other types of financial assistance.

SEEKING YOUR CAREER

When you are ready to start your job search consider the following suggestions:

Read one or two books on how to find a job. Ask your school or public librarian for recommendations and check the suggested readings in Appendix A.

If you are still in school or college, ask the guidance counselor or someone in the college personnel office for job leads and advice.

Tell everyone you know about your job hunting goal because they may hear of openings.

Register at your state employment security office and at private employment agencies. (See the list of state offices in the white pages of your telephone directory for the nearest employment security office, and in the yellow pages turn to the heading, "Employment Agencies.")

Study the help-wanted advertisements in your local newspapers.

Visit the offices of transport operators where you hope to find work and ask if you may file an application. Write to the out-of-town companies.

Finally, don't become discouraged. Keep up your search every day. Remember that you *will* find a job if you look hard enough.

FIVE CAREER TIPS FOR THE 21ST CENTURY

In 1996 Labor Secretary Robert Reich gave the following career tips to the millions of young men and women graduating from schools and colleges:

1. Regardless of whether you clean the office or work at a desk, become computer literate.
2. Continue your education after graduation to keep your skills sharp.

3. Catch on to the Web. Earn more money from your expertise, not from accumulating seniority.
4. Network with others in your specialty or profession to sharpen your skills.
5. Tomorrow's workers will function as teammates. Therefore learn to handle all the positions on the team and win as a team, not as an individual.

"You can be anything you want to be. But wanting to be isn't enough. Dreaming about it isn't enough. You've got to study for it, work for it, fight for it with all your heart and soul." (Colin L. Powell. *My American Journey.*)

THE FUTURE IS YOURS

Few industries offer the variety of job opportunities that transportation does. Most importantly transportation is a business that places an awesome responsibility on you. For example, a nut that is not properly tightened, an underinflated tire, or a restraining block of wood not removed from a wing joint could be the cause of tragedy. During the years ahead, the lives of many men, women, and children could depend on how carefully and conscientiously you perform your duties. As you can see, this is a career not to be undertaken lightly.

Whatever your decision, we wish you success in your chosen career.

APPENDIX A

SUGGESTED READINGS

The following books should prove interesting and helpful to anyone who wants further information about transportation careers. You may find additional current information about transportation in magazines and journals. We suggest that you consult the *Reader's Guide to Periodical Literature* and the *Business Periodicals Index,* which list all articles that have appeared in several dozen leading magazines. These indexes are easy to use and can be found in many public libraries.

Camenson, Blythe. *Travel.* VGM Career Portraits Series. Lincolnwood, IL: National Textbook Company, 1995.

Cudahy, Brian J. *Cash, Tokens, and Transfers: A History of Urban Mass Transit in North America.* New York: Fordham University Press, 1990.

De La Pedraja Toman, Rene. *The Rise and Decline of U.S. Merchant Shipping in the Twentieth Century.* New York: Macmillan Co, 1992.

Dunlop, Reginald. *Come Fly with Me: Your Nineties Guide to Becoming a Professional Flight Attendant.* Chicago: Maximillian Publishing, 1992.

Eberts, Marjorie and Martha. *Cars.* VGM Career Portraits Series. Lincolnwood, IL: National Textbook Company, 1995.

Finch, Christopher. *Highways to Heaven: The Auto Biography of America.* New York: Harper Collins, 1992.

Ford. VGM's Business Portrait Series. Lincolnwood, IL: National Textbook Company, 1996.

Friedheim, Eric. *Travel Agents: From Caravans and Clippers to the Concorde.* New York: Drake Publishers, 1992.

Historical Survey of Transit Buses in the United States. New York: Society of Automotive Engineers, 1990.

Holbrook, Stewart H. *The Story of American Railroads.* New York: Crown Publishers. (Considered a classic on this subject.)

I Can Be an Airline Pilot. New York: Outlet Book Company, 1992.

Krueger, Gretchen Dewailly. *Opportunities in Petroleum Careers.* Lincolnwood, IL: National Textbook Company, 1990.

Leary, William M., editor. *The Airline Industry.* New York: Facts on File, 1992.

Martin, Albro. *Railroads Triumphant: The Growth, Rejection, and Rebirth of a Vital American Force.* New York: Columbia University Press, 1992.

Milne, Robert. *Opportunities in Travel Careers.* Lincolnwood, IL: National Textbook Company, 1996.

Morrison, Tom. *To Fly Through the Air: The Experiences of Learning to Fly.* Ames, IA: Iowa State University Press, 1991.

Paradis, Adrian A. *Opportunities in Airline Careers.* Lincolnwood, IL: National Textbook Company, 1997.

————. *Opportunities in Military Careers.* Lincolnwood, IL: National Textbook Company, 1989.

Perry, Philip. *Opportunities in Automotive Services.* Lincolnwood, IL: National Textbook Company, 1996.

Petras, Kathryn and Ross. *Jobs '96.* New York: Simon & Schuster, 1995. (Excellent reference book listing leading companies, industry associations, directories, and periodicals for automotive industry, aviation, railroads, shipping, travel, and trucking.)

Plawin, Paul. *Careers for Travel Buffs and Other Restless Types.* Lincolnwood, IL: National Textbook Company, 1992.

Reed, Dan. *The American Eagle: The Ascent of Bob Crandall and American Airlines.* New York: St. Martins Press, 1993.

Scharnberg, Ken. *Opportunities in Trucking.* Lincolnwood, IL: National Textbook Company, 1992.

Weber, Robert. *Opportunities in Automotive Service.* Lincolnwood, IL: National Textbook Company, 1989.

PRINCIPAL TRANSPORTATION LABOR UNIONS

Air Line Employees Association, International
  5600 South Central Avenue
  Chicago, IL 60638

Air Line Pilots Association
  1625 Massachusetts Avenue, NW
  Washington, DC 20036

Aircraft Mechanics Fraternal Association
  P.O. Box 39
  Fayetteville, GA 30214

Allied Pilots Association
  P.O. Box 5524
  Arlington, TX 76005

Amalgamated Transit Union
  5025 Wisconsin Avenue, NW
  Washington, DC 20016

American Train Dispatchers Association
  1370 Ontario Street
  Cleveland, OH 44113

Association of Flight Attendants
  1625 Massachusetts Avenue, NW
  Washington, DC 20036

Brotherhood of Locomotive Engineers
  1370 Ontario Street
  Cleveland, OH 44113-1703

Brotherhood of Maintenance of Way Employees
  26555 Evergreen Road
  Southfield, MI 48076-4235

Brotherhood of Railroad Signalmen
  601 West Golf Road
  Mt. Prospect, IL 60056

Brotherhood of the Railway Carmen
  3 Research Place
  Rockville, MD 20850

Flight Engineers International Association
  1926 South Pacific Coast Highway, No. 202
  Redondo Beach, CA 90277-6145

International Brotherhood of Teamsters
  25 Louisiana Avenue, NW
  Washington, DC 20001

International Longshoremen's and Warehousemen's Union
  1188 Franklin Street
  San Francisco, CA 94109

International Longshoremen's Association
  17 Battery Place
  New York, NY 10004

International Organization of Masters, Mates and Pilots
  700 Maritime Boulevard
  Linthicum Heights, MD 21090

International Union, United Automobile, Aerospace and Agricultural
    Implement Workers of America
  8000 East Jefferson
  Detroit, MI 48214

Marine Engineers' Beneficial Association/National Maritime Union
  1125 Fifteenth Street, NW
  Washington, DC 20005

Pacific Coast Marine Firemen, Oilers, Watertenders and Wipers Association
  240 Second Street
  San Francisco, CA 94105

National Association of Air Traffic Specialists
  Wheaton Plaza North
  Wheaton, MD 20902

Seafarers International Union of North America
    5201 Auth Way
    Camp Springs, MD 20746

Transport Workers Union of America
    80 West End Avenue
    New York, NY 10023

Transportation Communication International Union
    3 Research Place
    Rockville, MD 20850

United Transportation Union
    14600 Detroit Avenue
    Lakewood, OH 44107-4250

CAREER STATISTICS FOR SELECTED TRANSPORTATION JOBS

Except as noted, all statistics presented here are the latest compiled by the U.S. Bureau of Labor Statistics as published in the 1996–1997 edition of its *Occupational Outlook Handbook*. Annual average or median earnings are included wherever available; some data are presented as weekly or hourly rates. Initials following salaries denote annual (a), weekly (w), and hourly (h) figures. The last numerals refer to the job outlook up to the year 2005 as defined below:

1. Grows much faster than the average (increases 36 percent or more)
2. Grows faster than the average (increases 21–35 percent)
3. Grows about as fast as the average (increases 10–20 percent)
4. Grows more slowly than the average or little or no change (increases 0–9 percent)
5. Declines (decreases 1 percent or more)

Accounting clerk—$19,500, a, 4

Advertising manager—$25,000, a, 2

Air traffic controller—$59,800, a, 4

Aircraft mechanic (average starting salary in 1993)—$8.70 to $15.56 per hour for applicant with A&P training (courtesy of FAPA*), 3

Automotive mechanic—$439, w, 3

Billing, cost and rate clerk—$19,500, a, 4

Billing, posting, and calculating machine operator—$17,800, a, 4

Bookkeeper and accounting clerk—$19,000, a, 4

Bus driver—$16.74, h (companies with more than 1,000 employees), $14.39, h (companies with fewer than 1,000 employees), 3

Buyer and purchaser—$31,700, a, 4

Captain (airline)—Average ALPA captain forty-eight years of age, has twenty years service, earns about $110,000; a (courtesy ALPA**), 3

Captain (water vessels)—$684, w, 4

Chef, cook, and other kitchen worker—$6.85, h, (executive chef, $40,000), 3

Computer operator—$21,300, a, 5

Computer programmer—$38,000, a, 3

Computer systems analyst—$44,000, a, 1

Customs inspector—$39,000, a, 3

Data entry keyer—$17,600, a, 4

Diesel mechanic—$14.61, h, 3

Dispatcher—$402, w, 4

Duplicating, mail, and other office machine operator—4

Economist and marketing research analyst—$27,600 (degree in economics), $25,400 (degree in marketing), a, 1

Employment interviewer—1

File clerk—$16,200, a, 4

First officer (copilot)—Average ALPA first officer, forty years of age, ten years' service, earns about $58,000, a, 3. Starting salaries range from $10,000–$24,000 depending on size of aircraft flown (courtesy ALPA)

Flight attendant—$10,872 to $14,766 for turboprop aircraft, $14,796 for jet aircraft (average starting salaries in 1993), a, 1 (courtesy FAPA)

Flight engineer—Average ALPA flight engineer, thirty-seven years of age with six years' service, earns about $38,000, a, 3 (courtesy ALPA)

Food preparation worker—$6.00–$8.00, h, 3

General maintenance mechanic—$9.40, h, 3

General office clerk—$19,300, a, 4

Guard—$6.00, h, 2

Labor relations specialist—$25,800, a (bachelor's degree), $38,700, a (master's degree), 1

Locomotive engineer—$47,000–$62,900, a, 4

Mail clerk—$322, w, 5

Mate—$684, w, 4

Material moving equipment operator—$459, w, 4

Meteorologist—$22,000, a (bachelor's degree), $27,000, a (master's degree), $37,000, a (Ph.D. degree), 4

Officer (Great Lakes Ships)—starting salary approximately $80–$110 per day plus benefits, 4

Ordinary seaman—$533, w, 5

Parking lot attendant—$311, w, 3

Payroll clerk—$21,300, a, 4

Precision instrument repairers—4

Public relations specialist—$23,000, a, 3

Receptionist—3

Reservations clerk—4

Seaman—$533, w, 5

Secretary—$26,700, a, 4

Service station attendant—$311, w, 3

Shipping and receiving clerk—4

Statistician—$56,890, a (in federal government), 4

Statistical clerk—4

Stenographer—$399, w, 4

Stockroom clerk—4

Taxi driver—$375, w, 1

Telephone operator—$398, w, 5

Ticket agent—4

Tire repairer—4

Travel agent—$21,000, a, 1

Truck driver—$12.73, h (long-distance drivers, $20,000–$40,000, a), 3

Typist—$17,000, a, 4

Vehicle washer and equipment cleaner—$311, w, 3

Word processor—$22,900, a, 4

---

*Formerly the Future Airline Professionals of America

**Air Line Pilots Association

APPENDIX D

CANADIAN TRANSPORTATION INFORMATION SOURCES

Air Traffic Services: For information call 1–800–667–4636. Canada's air navigation system was scheduled to be transferred at some point to Nav Canada. Transport Canada has been responsible for training in air traffic services.

Bus Transportation: For information on careers in bus transportation, contact the Canadian Urban Transit Association at Suite 901, 55 York Street, Toronto, Ontario M5J 1R7.

Canadian Domestic and International Airlines: See *Opportunities in Airline Careers,* Lincolnwood, IL: VGM Career Horizons, 1996.

Canadian Regulatory and Airport Authorities: Transport Canada, Assistant Deputy Minister, Safety and Security, 330 Sparks Street, 12th Floor, Ottawa, Ontario K1A 0N8; Transport Canada, Assistant Deputy Minister, Airports, 330 Sparks Street, 19th Floor, Ottawa, Ontario K1A 0N8.

Local Transportation Services: Inquire at the employment office of the principal office.

Marine Transportation: The Canadian Coast Guard offers information about training in the field of marine transportation. Contact the Coast Guard at the Department of Fisheries and Oceans, Ottawa, Ontario K1A 0N7.

Rail Transportation: The three major railroad companies are: Canadian National Railway Co., 935 de la Gauchetière St. W., Montreal, Quebec H3C 3N4; Canadian Pacific Railway Co., Windsor Station, Room 227, Montreal, Quebec, H3C 3E4; VIA Rail Canada, Inc., 2 Place Ville-Marie, Montreal, Quebec H3C 3N3.

Web Site: You may visit Transport Canada's Web site at http://www.tc.gc.ca/.